The
PALEO COMFORT FOODS BIBLE

ANNA CONRAD

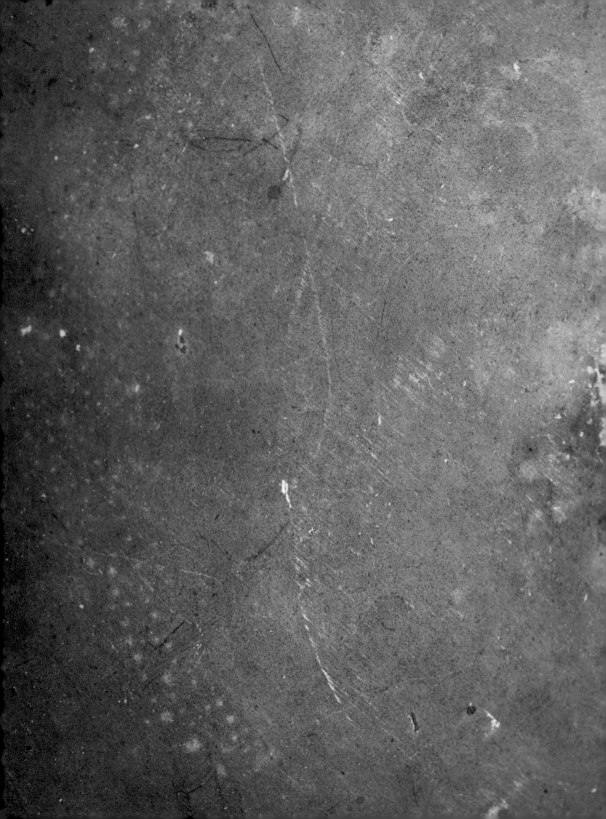

The
PALEO COMFORT FOODS BIBLE

ANNA CONRAD

Photography by
J. STANFIELD PHOTOGRAPHY

Skyhorse Publishing

Dedicated to James Caldwell and Joseph Conrad, who inspired me to create delicious dinners with their smiles and words of encouragement.

Notice

This book is intended as a reference volume only, not as a medical manual. The information given here is designed to help you make informed decisions about your health. It is not intended as a substitute for any treatment that may have been prescribed by your doctor. If you suspect that you may have medical problems, we urge you to seek competent medical help.

{ Contents }

{ Welcome }

Welcome to *The Paleo Comfort Foods Bible*. I wrote, tested, and edited the recipes in this book in my kitchen, located in Chattanooga, Tennessee. My mission with *The Paleo Comfort Foods Bible* is to create a comprehensive collection of favorite comfort food recipes and reformulate them to comply as closely as possible with the paleo diet. I garnered feedback from family, friends, and customers to create the recipes in this book. In many, many instances the recipes are better when converted to paleo versions. I hope you enjoy the recipes, many of which you will recognize as all-time favorites. And hopefully you will consider the paleo versions to be even better than the old recipe you remember.

{ Preface }

The paleo diet does not lend itself to easily incorporating traditional comfort food recipes into the everyday menu. However, I believe you'll find that *The Paleo Comfort Foods Bible* includes recipes that evoke warm feelings, full stomachs, and feelings of home without grains, dairy, and high glycemic index sugar products. Pasta, breadcrumbs, cheese, cream, and sugar often find their way into comfort food recipes. I've reformulated these recipes to incorporate breads made with nut flours and paleo-safe oils and sugars. Pasta is more of a challenge, and even the "paleo pastas" on the market didn't pass my criteria as a paleo-friendly food. For that reason, I don't include pasta in my recipes. If the recipe requires a pasta-like ingredient, I use spaghetti squash. You will not miss the pasta! When choosing ingredients for the recipes in this book, make sure you always use high-quality, organic, grass–fed meat and poultry, wild-caught seafood and fish, uncured meats (unless you cure them via paleo-friendly methods), whole foods, and additive-free ingredients whenever possible. For a complete list of foods allowed on the paleo diet, see my first cookbook, *The Paleo Cookbook*.

{ Stocking Your Pantry }

The following is a list of standard ingredients you will need to have in your pantry before making the recipes in this book, in addition to commonly used ingredients. I've listed suppliers for almond flour because almond flour is the key ingredient in many of the recipes, and the suppliers I list here are the best brands to use, based on my experience. I did not list suppliers for other ingredients because I found that they are widely available from multiple suppliers without much variation in quality.

ALMOND FLOUR AND ALMOND MEAL: Almond flour and almond meal are made by grinding sweet almonds. Almond flour is finely ground blanched almonds. Blanching almonds removes the skin. Almond meal is made with or without the skin on the almonds, and it isn't as finely ground as almond flour. The consistency of almond meal is similar to that of corn meal. I used almond flour from three different suppliers and found them all to be acceptable in my recipes. The almond flour suppliers I used are JK Gourmet (www.jkgourmet.com), Benefit Your Life (www.benefityourlifestore.com), and Honeyville (www.honeyvillegrain.com). I grind my own almond meal from whole almonds since I use it smaller quantities.

COCONUT FLOUR: Coconut flour is the meat of a coconut ground finely and defatted. When purchasing, make sure the ingredients state pure coconut flour without any added ingredients such as rice flour, sugars, or preservatives. Choose coconut flours that are not pristine white in color because that may indicate unnecessary processing. The color should be similar to coconut flesh, a little off-white and cream-colored.

COCONUT OIL: Coconut oil is extracted from the coconut flesh (meat). Coconut oil is used in many paleo recipes and is the primary fat used in this cookbook. Choose virgin coconut oil (VCO) that is made from fresh coconut and mechanically pressed to extract the oil. Other forms of coconut oil may be extracted via chemical or high temperature methods, which can reduce the nutrient content and flavor properties of the oil.

OLIVE OIL: Vegetable oils are typically off-limits for paleo dieters, and olive oil is vegetable oil. However, it's considered paleo-friendly because it is comprised mostly of monounsaturated fat, a fat source that is safe and healthy for us to consume. It is not suitable for cooking with on the stovetop or for greasing pans for baking because it oxidizes at higher temperatures, breaking down into compounds that aren't healthy for humans to consume. Use it in dressings or on top of your already cooked meals.

Fresh, cold-pressed, extra virgin olive oils in dark bottles that haven't been on the shelf for a long time are the best. Store olive oil in a dark and cool place to increase its shelf life. You can store it in the refrigerator, but it will become cloudy and thick. Refrigerated olive oil will return to its normal appearance and consistency once it comes to room temperature.

RENDERED ANIMAL FAT: They are the essence of the reason we eat paleo in the first place. Cavemen ate animals—lots of them—for energy, and therefore they obtained a lot of fat from animal sources.

Most animal fats are highly saturated and are therefore stable enough to cook at high temperatures. Conversely, they are solid at room temperature and don't need to be refrigerated. Their reputation for being "less healthy" means that they are not very popular, and therefore very cheap to obtain—even the fats coming from well-treated animals.

Just go to your butcher and ask for duck fat, pork lard, or beef tallow. Your butcher might not have those fats rendered and ready for you to cook, so you'll have to work a bit to use them, but you'll see that it's not terribly difficult. You may also purchase leaf lard or suet (beef fat).

DRY METHOD OF RENDERING ANIMAL FAT

Remove any vein, meat, or blood from the fat, and then chop it into very small chunks. Next put the fat chunks in either a crockpot or heavy-bottomed Dutch oven. Set the fat over very low heat. Once all the white fat chunks have become brown and dry, strain off the pure fat and let it cool. Be careful, as it will be very hot. Once cooled, the fat will be white and hard at room temperature. You are ready to cook with real animal fat!

COCONUT MILK: Coconut milk is the liquid that comes from squeezing the meat of fresh coconut. Coconut milk can be thick or thin depending on the fat content or whether or not a thickener has been added. Canned coconut milk is often diluted with water to achieve a lower fat content. Light coconut milk is the lowest fat-containing coconut milk. The recipes in this book are made with canned coconut milk with a 20 to 22 percent fat content (not light). If possible, choose coconut milk that contains no additional ingredients, other than water. Thickeners such as guar gum are often added and should be avoided if at all possible. You can make your own coconut milk by purchasing a fresh coconut, shredding the meat, and processing the flesh in a food processor with water. Use 4 cups of hot water and 2 cups of shredded coconut. After processing, pour the milk through a strainer to remove the coconut. Use immediately or store the strained milk in the refrigerator for 3-4 days.

VINEGAR: Vinegars that are naturally fermented at home or by a local artisan are the best sources of vinegar to use in your cooking. You may also find naturally fermented vinegars in a local health food store or at your local farmer's market. You may even be lucky enough to find naturally fermented vinegar for sale online if none of the local options are available to you. I do not recommend using industrially processed vinegars because they typically contain industrially processed acetic acid, which is not considered to be paleo-friendly. Good quality apple cider, red wine, and balsamic vinegars are easiest to find and specified most often in my recipes. You can also make your own vinegar from the further fermentation of mead (fermentation of raw honey, water, and sometimes fruit). There are many recipes online that can help you get started.

BAKING SODA: Baking soda (sodium bicarbonate) is used in baking as a leavening agent when acidic ingredients are present. Acidic ingredients include phosphates, cream of tartar, lemon juice, yogurt, buttermilk, cacao powder, vinegar, etc. Baking soda reacts with the acidic ingredient and releases carbon dioxide, causing the baked good to rise. Baking soda is often used in combination with baking powder.

BAKING POWDER: Baking powder is a leavening agent composed of a weak acid and a weak base that allows baked goods to rise via an acid-base reaction. Baking powder is used in breads where a fermentation reaction (via yeast) is undesirable because of the taste fermentation imparts. Baked goods or breads that use baking powder to create "lift" in the baked good are often called quick breads because of the quick release of carbon dioxide in the acid-base reaction, yielding shorter processing times (no waiting for the bread to rise before baking).

EGGS: Eggs play a critical role in baking by providing protein, fat, and moisture. Protein acts as a binding agent to keep the baked good in one piece and breading in place, rather than crumbling. Fat and moisture provides an excellent mouth-feel and makes the baked good consumable and pleasant to eat, versus dry and hard to chew or swallow. The recipes in this book use more eggs in many of the recipes than most non-paleo recipes might, especially when coconut flour is incorporated, because the nut flours tend to absorb more moisture than a traditional grain-based flour. Use eggs from free-range chickens or other game birds when possible. The nutrient profile for free-range birds is more paleo-friendly than those purchased from mass-production farming facilities.

TAPIOCA FLOUR AND ARROWROOT FLOUR: Tapioca flour is derived from cassava root and can be used to make breads and tortillas as the primary flour component, breading for meat and vegetables, and as a thickening agent to replace cornstarch or other grain-based thickeners. Arrowroot flour is often used interchangeably with tapioca flour and is acceptable for the paleo diet. I used tapioca flour in the recipes in this book in an attempt to minimize the number of ingredients in my pantry. I also found tapioca flour to be a little less expensive than arrowroot flour. Do not confuse tapioca pearls with tapioca flour for the purpose of the recipes in this book. Purchase the tapioca in flour form and check the ingredients to make sure it isn't adulterated with wheat flour. Both tapioca and arrowroot flours are starches and should be used only when needed. Comfort food recipes include some starches for mouth-feel, primarily, and just wouldn't be the same without them. I've tried to keep the quantities used to an absolute minimum. If a recipe calls for starch to be a major component of the meal—tortillas, for example—just make sure you aren't preparing the recipe more than once or twice each month. Starches trigger carbohydrate cravings, so be aware that you may want more starches than usual and plan to resist! The craving will pass in a few hours.

HONEY: Honey is a sweetener created by bees, which derive the thick fluid by eating flower nectar and processing it until it dehydrates the sugar and creates natural monosaccharide, fructose, and glucose, with a flavor similar in sweetness to granulated white sugar. Because honey has a low water content, most harmful microorganisms will not grow in it. However, honey may contain dormant endospores that are harmful to the immature intestinal tract of infants, which can cause serious illness or even death. For that reason, honey should not be included in recipes that will be eaten by infants. When possible purchase raw, locally produced honey, for both environmental reasons and because locally harvested honey will have the flavor of local nectar. Raw honey has a significantly lower glycemic index and higher nutrient content than commercially produced and packaged honey. If you cannot tolerate raw honey or if you will be feeding the baked good to an infant, consider real maple sugar or blackstrap molasses as a substitute although the flavor profile will vary when using different sugars. Maple syrup is milder, and blackstrap molasses have a more robust in flavor.

BLACKSTRAP MOLASSES: Blackstrap molasses is a by-product of the manufacture of granulated sugar or cane sugar. The syrup's flavor, thickness, and nutritional content vary depending upon whether it's the product of the second or third boiling steps during manufacturing. The first boiling product in sugar manufacture is "cane syrup," not blackstrap molasses. The second boiling is called second molasses, which has a slightly bitter flavor. The third boiling produces blackstrap molasses, which is famous for its robust flavor. Blackstrap molasses contains calcium, magnesium, potassium, and iron. One tablespoon of blackstrap molasses is reputed to contain 20 percent of the daily nutritional value for each of these nutrients. Blackstrap molasses is used in many of the recipes in this book.

PALM SUGAR: Palm sugar is a nutrient-rich, unrefined, low-glycemic, natural sweetener that is obtained by making several slits in the stem of a palm tree, draining the liquid, and then boiling it until thickened. The boiled product is cooled into cakes and later ground and packaged for sale. Palm sugar is a rich brown color, and some say its taste is superior to that of white granulated sugar. Palm sugar behaves much the same as white granulated sugar in baking applications. Palm sugar is not the same as coconut sugar, which is obtained from the cut flowers of the coconut palm tree. The recipes in this book use palm sugar.

The
PALEO COMFORT FOODS BIBLE

ANNA CONRAD

{ Comfort Food Recipes }

Vegetable Sides

Casseroles and One-Dish Meals

{ Starters and Quick Bites }

Buffalo Wings

Ingredients

3 pounds chicken wings, halved at joint and wingtips removed, trimmed

1 tablespoon baking powder

½ teaspoon sea salt

⅔ cup Louisiana-Style Fermented Hot Pepper Sauce (see page 226)

1 tablespoon coconut oil, melted

1 tablespoon blackstrap molasses

Preparation

1. Adjust oven rack to middle position and preheat oven to 475° F. Line a rimmed baking sheet with aluminum foil and top with a wire rack. Pat wings dry with paper towels, then toss with baking powder and sea salt in a bowl. Arrange wings in a single layer on wire rack. Roast wings until golden on both sides, about 40 minutes, flipping wings over and rotating sheet halfway through roasting.

2. While the wings are cooking, whisk pepper sauce, oil, and blackstrap molasses together in large bowl.

3. Remove wings from oven. Adjust oven rack to a position six inches from broiler element and heat broiler. Broil wings until golden brown on both sides, 6 to 8 minutes, flipping wings over halfway through broiling. Add wings to sauce and toss to coat. Serve.

Coconut Shrimp with Orange Dipping Sauce

SERVES 6

Ingredients

Orange Dipping Sauce
¾ cup orange juice (2 oranges)

¼ cup apricot jam (see page 98)

1 tablespoon honey

2 teaspoons tapioca or arrowroot starch

Pinch ground ginger

Pinch garlic powder

Lemon juice, freshly squeezed

Sea salt

Coconut Shrimp
1¾ cups White Sandwich Breadcrumbs (see page 19)

1 tablespoon coconut oil

⅓ cup unsweetened shredded coconut

⅓ cup tapioca or arrowroot flour

2 large eggs

½ teaspoon sea salt

¼ teaspoon cayenne pepper

Olive oil spray or coconut oil for greasing rack

1½ pounds extra-large shrimp, wild-caught, peeled and deveined

Preparation

1. **For the Orange Dipping Sauce:** Whisk juice, jam, honey, flour, ginger, and garlic powder together in small saucepan. Bring to a simmer over medium-high heat, whisking constantly. Reduce heat to medium-low and simmer gently, whisking often, until slightly thickened, 3 to 5 minutes. Remove from heat, season with lemon juice and sea salt to taste; allow to cool.

2. **For the Coconut Shrimp:** Adjust oven rack to middle position and preheat oven to 475° F. Toss breadcrumbs with oil, spread onto a rimmed baking sheet, and bake until lightly golden, about 7 minutes. Stir in coconut and continue to bake until crumbs and coconut are a deep golden color, about 2 minutes longer. Allow to cool slightly.

3. Spread flour into a shallow dish. In a second shallow dish, lightly beat eggs until foamy. In a third shallow dish, combine the breadcrumb and coconut mixture with sea salt and cayenne. Line a rimmed baking sheet with aluminum foil, top with a wire rack, and grease the rack with coconut oil.

4. Pat shrimp dry with paper towels. Working with several shrimp at a time, dredge in flour, dip in the eggs, and then coat with the breadcrumb mixture, pressing gently to adhere. Lay the shrimp on the prepared wire rack. Bake shrimp until just cooked through, about 5 to 7 minutes. Serve with Orange Dipping Sauce.

Chef's Note: Shrimp come in a variety of sizes and are typically identified by count per pound. Use this chart to determine which shrimp to purchase for the recipe. Shrimp per pound:

- 10 shrimp or less = Colossal
- 11 to 15 = Jumbo
- 16 to 20 = Extra-large
- 21 to 30 = Large
- 31 to 35 = Medium
- 36 to 45 = Small
- about 100 = Miniature

Herbed Deviled Eggs

SERVES 6

Ingredients

6 large eggs

2 tablespoons Mayonnaise (see page 214)

1 tablespoon minced fresh parsley, chives, or cilantro

1 tablespoon warm tap water

½ teaspoon white wine vinegar

½ teaspoon Dijon Mustard (see page 225)

⅛ teaspoon turmeric

⅛ teaspoon ground coriander

⅛ teaspoon sea salt

⅛ teaspoon pepper

Preparation

1. Place eggs in a medium saucepan, cover with one inch of water, and bring to a boil over high heat. Remove the pan from heat, cover, and let stand for 10 minutes. Fill a large bowl with ice water. Pour off the water from the saucepan and gently shake the pan back and forth to lightly crack shells. Transfer the eggs to the ice water and allow to cool for 5 minutes, then peel.

2. Cut eggs in half lengthwise. Remove the yolks from the egg whites and place in a bowl. Place whites on a serving platter. Add Mayonnaise, parsley, water, vinegar, Dijon Mustard, turmeric, coriander, sea salt, and pepper to the yolks and break up the yolks with a spatula or fork until smooth and well combined.

3. Transfer mixture to a pastry bag fitted with a star tip (or zipper storage bag with one corner snipped off) and pipe yolk mixture into whites. Cover and refrigerate until chilled, at least two hours and up to one day.

Curried Stuffed Eggs

Ingredients

12 large eggs

2 tablespoons Mayonnaise (see page 214)

2 tablespoons finely minced Peach Chutney (page 11)

1 teaspoon white wine vinegar

1 teaspoon curry powder

1 teaspoon sea salt

2 tablespoons minced red onion

2 tablespoons minced celery

1 tablespoon chopped fresh Italian parsley and/or dash of paprika, for garnish

Preparation

1. Place eggs in a medium saucepan, cover with one inch of water, and bring to a boil over high heat. Remove pan from the heat, cover, and let stand for 10 minutes. Fill a large bowl with ice water. Pour off the water from the saucepan and gently shake the pan back and forth to lightly crack shells. Transfer the eggs to the ice water, allow to cool for 5 minutes, then peel.

2. Cut eggs in half lengthwise. Remove the yolks from the egg whites. Place whites on a serving platter. Combine egg yolks, Mayonnaise, vinegar, curry powder, and sea salt and stir until smooth, breaking up the yolks with a spatula or fork until smooth and well combined.

3. Stir the onion, celery, and parsley into yolk mixture. Pipe the egg yolk mixture evenly into the egg white halves. Arrange on a serving platter and top each egg with a small dollop of peach chutney. Cover and refrigerate until chilled, at least two hours and up to one day.

Peach Chutney

MAKES 2½ PINTS

Ingredients

4 pounds firm, ripe peaches or 3½ pounds frozen peaches, no additives

1⅔ cups palm sugar

1 cup apple cider vinegar

2 tablespoons ginger root, minced

1 small red onion, slivered

12 cardamom pods, lightly cracked

2 to 4 dried hot red chilies, seeded, stemmed, and thinly sliced

Sea salt, to taste

Ice water bath

Preparation

1. Bring a large pot of water to a boil and fill a large bowl with ice water. Using a paring knife, score the bottom of each peach with a small X. Add the peaches to the boiling water for 30 seconds, and then transfer them to the ice water bath with a slotted spoon. When cool enough to handle, peel the peaches, then halve them and remove the pits. Dice the peaches into three-quarter-inch pieces.

2. In a medium, enameled cast-iron casserole pan over medium-high heat, combine the palm sugar with the vinegar, ginger, onion, and cardamom; stir to dissolve the sugar. Reduce heat to medium-low and simmer until the onion is slightly softened, about 8 minutes. Add the peaches, chilies, and a pinch of sea salt and simmer over medium-low heat, stirring occasionally, until the peaches are very soft and translucent, about one hour.

3. Ladle the chutney into five half-pint canning jars, tapping each jar lightly on a flat surface to release any air bubbles. Seal the jars and refrigerate for up to six months.

Stuffed Eggs with Lacto-Fermented Horseradish

SERVES 8

Ingredients

12 large eggs

2 tablespoons Mayonnaise (see page 214)

1 tablespoon Lacto-Fermented Horseradish, drained (see page 226)

1 teaspoon white wine vinegar

1 teaspoon Dijon Mustard (see page 225)

¼ teaspoon sea salt

2 tablespoons minced red onion

2 tablespoons minced celery

1 tablespoon chopped fresh Italian parsley

Paprika or parsley for garnish

Preparation

1. Place the eggs in a large saucepan and fill with cold water. Cover pot and bring water to a boil over medium heat. Turn off the heat and let the eggs stand for 10 minutes. Peel eggs under cold running water.

2. Cut the eggs in half lengthwise. Remove the egg yolks from the egg whites. Place egg whites on serving platter. Combine the egg yolk, Mayonnaise, Lacto-Fermented Horseradish, vinegar, Dijon Mustard, and sea salt, breaking up the egg yolks with a spatula or fork and until smooth. and well combined.

3. Stir the onion, celery, and parsley into the egg yolk mixture. Pipe the egg yolk mixture evenly into the egg white halves. Arrange on a serving platter. Cover and refrigerate until chilled, at least two hours and up to one day. Sprinkle with paprika just before serving.

Cheesy Garlic Bread

SERVES 8

Ingredients

5 garlic cloves, minced

1 tablespoons coconut oil

1 tablespoon plus ½ teaspoon water

½ cup Mayonnaise **(see page 214)**

¼ teaspoon pepper

1 recipe White Sandwich Bread baked in French bread loaf pan (see page 19)

6 ounces shredded Coconut Milk Cheddar Cheese (see page 239)

Preparation

1. Adjust oven rack to the lower-middle position and preheat oven to 400° F. Cook garlic, coconut oil, and ½ teaspoon water together in eight-inch nonstick skillet over low heat, stirring occasionally, until garlic is sticky and straw-colored, about 7 to 10 minutes. Transfer to bowl; stir in Mayonnaise, pepper, and remaining one tablespoon water.

2. Using a serrated knife, slice loaf in half horizontally, then score interior crumb crosswise at one-inch intervals, about three-quarters of an inch deep; do not cut through crust. Spread garlic mixture over cut sides of bread.

3. Sandwich bread halves back together and wrap in aluminum foil. Place on baking sheet; bake for 15 minutes. Unwrap bread and lay, cut sides up, on baking sheet. Continue to bake until just beginning to brown, about 10 minutes longer. Remove bread from oven. Adjust oven rack to a position eight inches from the broiler element and heat broiler.

4. Sprinkle cheese over cut sides of bread; broil until the cheese has melted and the edges of the bread are crisp, 1 to 2 minutes. Transfer bread, cheese side up, to a cutting board and, using a serrated knife, cut evenly into sixteen pieces. Serve.

{ Soups, Sandwiches, and Salads }

White Sandwich Bread

MAKES 1 NINE-INCH LOAF

Ingredients

1 cup warm coconut milk	1½ cups coconut flour and ½ cup extra if needed
3 tablespoons coconut oil, melted and cooled	1 tablespoon baking powder
2 tablespoons honey	2 teaspoons salt
2 cups almond flour	Extra coconut oil for greasing loaf pan.

Preparation

1. Preheat oven to 350° F. Grease a 9x5-inch loaf pan with coconut oil.
2. Mix all dry ingredients together in a bowl and whisk to combine.
3. Mix all wet ingredients together in a second bowl and whisk to combine.
4. Add wet ingredients to dry ingredients and whisk to combine.
5. Scrape the dough into the prepared loaf pan using a rubber spatula. Bake until golden brown, 20 to 30 minutes, rotating the loaf halfway through baking. Cool the loaf in the pan for about 15 minutes, then flip out onto a wire rack and allow to cool to room temperature, up to two hours, before serving.

Chef's Note: You can use this bread to make breadcrumbs. Preheat oven to 350° F. Tear or cut bread into half-inch pieces and place in a single layer on a baking sheet. Place baking sheet in the oven and bake for 15 to 25 minutes, or until bread is dried out and no longer soft in the center. Check on bread at 10-minute intervals. Remove from oven and cool on a rack. Place cooled bread in a food processor and process until desired crumb size is reached. To make panko breadcrumbs, remove the crust from the bread before tearing into pieces.

Use this same technique to make croutons. Instead of tearing bread into pieces, cut the bread into quarter- to half-inch pieces. Consider tossing the croutons in your favorite herbs and spices before baking.

Hearty Sandwich Bread

MAKES 1 NINE-INCH LOAF

Ingredients

1 cup warm coconut milk

3 tablespoons coconut oil, melted and cooled, plus1 tablespoon extra for brushing

2 tablespoons honey

2 cups almond flour

1½ cups coconut flour and ½ cup extra if needed

1 tablespoon baking powder

2 teaspoons salt

2 tablespoons flaxseeds

Preparation

1. Preheat oven to 350° F. Grease a 9x5-inch loaf pan with coconut oil.
2. Mix all dry ingredients together in a bowl and whisk to combine.
3. Mix all wet ingredients together in a second bowl and whisk to combine.
4. Add wet ingredients to dry ingredients and whisk to combine.
5. Scrape the dough into the prepared loaf pan using a rubber spatula. Bake until golden brown, 20 to 30 minutes, rotating the loaf halfway through baking. Cool the loaf in the pan for about 15 minutes, then flip out onto a wire rack and allow to cool to room temperature, up to two hours, before serving.

Chef's Note: You can use this bread to make breadcrumbs. Preheat oven to 350° F. Tear or cut bread into half-inch pieces and place in a single layer on a baking sheet. Place baking sheet in the oven and bake for 15 to 25 minutes, or until bread is dried out and no longer soft in the center. Check on bread at 10-minute intervals. Remove from oven and cool on a rack. Place cooled bread in a food processor and process until desired crumb size is reached. To make panko breadcrumbs, remove the crust from the bread before tearing into pieces.

Use this same technique to make croutons. Instead of tearing bread into pieces, cut the bread into quarter- to half-inch pieces. Consider tossing the croutons in your favorite herbs and spices before baking.

Spinach Salad with Warm Bacon Dressing

SERVES 4

Ingredients

8 ounces (8 cups) baby spinach, fresh

3 tablespoons balsamic vinegar

½ teaspoon honey

Sea salt and pepper to taste

4 slices bacon, cut into ½-inch pieces

½ red onion, chopped fine

¼ cup Chicken Broth or Stock (see page 236)

1 small garlic clove, minced

2 large hard-cooked eggs, peeled and sliced (see page 7 for instructions on cooking and peeling eggs)

Preparation

1. Place spinach in a large bowl. In a small bowl, whisk vinegar, honey, a pinch of sea salt, and ¼ teaspoon pepper together until honey dissolves; set aside. Cook bacon in a twelve-inch nonstick skillet over medium-high heat until crisp, about 5 minutes; transfer to paper towel–lined plate.

2. Pour off all but one tablespoon of the fat left in skillet and add onion and broth, cooking over medium heat until onion is softened and liquid is thick and syrupy, about 2 minutes. Stir in garlic and cook until fragrant, 15 to 30 seconds.

3. Stir in vinegar mixture and warm through briefly, then pour over spinach; toss gently to coat. Divide salad among four plates and garnish with cooked bacon and eggs. Serve.

Caesar Salad

Ingredients

¼ cup olive oil

2 tablespoons white wine vinegar

2 canned anchovy fillets, drained

1 small garlic clove, chopped

½ teaspoon Dijon Mustard (see page 225)

½ teaspoon Worcestershire Sauce (see page 230)

¼ teaspoon sea salt

⅛ teaspoon freshly ground pepper

16 cups loosely packed torn romaine lettuce

1 cup homemade croutons made from White or Hearty Sandwich Bread (see pages 19 or 20)

Preparation

1. To make the dressing, combine the oil, vinegar, anchovies, garlic, Dijon Mustard, Worcestershire Sauce, sea salt, and pepper in a blender and process until smooth.
2. Place the lettuce in a large bowl. Add the dressing and croutons and toss to coat. Divide the salad evenly among eight plates and serve at once.

Classic Wedge Salad with Bacon and Creamy Coconut Milk Cheddar Cheese Dressing

SERVES 6

Ingredients

4 slices bacon, cut into ¼-inch pieces

⅓ cup coconut milk

⅓ cup Mayonnaise (see page 214)

3 tablespoons water

1 tablespoon white wine vinegar

¼ teaspoon garlic powder

¼ teaspoon dried parsley

¼ teaspoon sea salt

¼ teaspoon pepper

1 head iceberg lettuce (9 ounces), cored and cut into 6 wedges

3 tomatoes, cored and cut into wedges

Preparation

1. Cook bacon in a twelve-inch nonstick skillet over medium-high heat until crisp, about 5 minutes; transfer to a paper towel–lined plate.
2. Whisk together Mayonnaise, coconut milk, water, vinegar, garlic powder, dried parsley, sea salt, and pepper until well combined.
3. Divide iceberg wedges and tomatoes among six plates. Spoon dressing over top and garnish with bacon. Serve.

Buffalo Chicken Salad

SERVES 4

Ingredients

⅔ cup plain coconut milk

¼ cup Mayonnaise (see Condiments)

¼ teaspoon dried parsley

3 tablespoons water

1 tablespoon lemon juice, fresh squeezed

2 garlic cloves, minced

Sea salt and pepper to taste

½ cup Louisiana-Style Fermented Hot Pepper Sauce (see page 226)

1 tablespoon olive oil

1 tablespoon blackstrap molasses

½ cup almond meal

1 tablespoon tapioca or arrowroot starch

4 (6-ounce) boneless, skinless chicken breasts, trimmed of all visible fat

1 tablespoon coconut oil

3 romaine lettuce hearts (18 ounces), torn into bite-size pieces

3 celery ribs, sliced thin

2 carrots, peeled and shredded

Preparation

1. Whisk coconut milk, Mayonnaise, dried parsley, water, lemon juice, garlic, ¼ teaspoon sea salt, and ⅛ teaspoon pepper together in small bowl. In a separate bowl, whisk Louisiana-Style Fermented Hot Pepper Sauce, olive oil, and blackstrap molasses together.

2. Combine almond meal and tapioca or arrowroot starch in shallow dish. Pat chicken dry with paper towels and season with sea salt and pepper. Dredge chicken in almond meal mixture, pressing on coating to adhere. Heat coconut oil in twelve-inch nonstick skillet over medium-high heat until just shimmering. Add chicken and cook until well browned on first side, 6 to 8 minutes. Flip chicken, reduce heat to medium-low, and continue to cook until chicken registers 160° F, 6 to 8 minutes longer. Transfer chicken to carving board, allow to rest for 5 minutes, and then slice crosswise into half-inch-thick pieces.

3. Toss lettuce, celery, and carrots with dressing and divide among four plates. Gently coat the chicken, being careful not to remove the almond meal breading, with hot pepper sauce mixture and arrange on top of salads. Serve.

Beef Taco Salad

SERVES 4

Ingredients

Taco Meat

1 teaspoon coconut oil or Rendered Animal
    Fat (see page ix)

1 onion, chopped fine

2 tablespoons chili powder

3 garlic cloves, minced

1 pound ground beef

1 (8-ounce) can tomato sauce

½ cup Chicken Broth or Stock
    (see page 239)

2 teaspoons white balsamic vinegar

1 teaspoon palm sugar

Sea salt and pepper to taste

Salad

4 (10-inch) Tortillas (page 32)

Coconut oil or Rendered Animal Fat
    (see page ix)

2 romaine lettuce hearts (12 ounces),
    shredded

8 ounces cherry or grape tomatoes,
    quartered

2 scallions, sliced thin

¼ cup fresh cilantro, chopped

2 tablespoons lime juice, freshly squeezed

Sea salt and pepper to taste

Preparation

1. **For the Taco Meat:** Heat oil in twelve-inch nonstick skillet over medium-high heat until shimmering. Add onion and cook until softened, about 5 minutes. Stir in chili powder and garlic and cook until fragrant, about 30 seconds. Add ground beef and cook, breaking up meat with a wooden spoon, until almost cooked through but still slightly pink, about 2 minutes. Stir in tomato sauce, broth, vinegar, and sugar and simmer until slightly thickened, about 5 minutes; mixture will be saucy. Remove from heat and season with sea salt and pepper to taste.

2. **For the Salad:** Adjust oven racks to the upper-middle and lower-middle positions and preheat oven to 425° F. Arrange four oven-safe soup bowls (or four slightly flattened, three-inch aluminum foil balls) upside down on two rimmed baking sheets. Place Tortillas on plate, cover with a damp paper towel, and microwave until warm and pliable, about 15 to 30 seconds.

3. Drape Tortillas over soup bowls, pressing the tops flat and pinching the sides to create a four-sided bowl. Bake until Tortillas are crisp, 10 to 15 minutes, switching and rotating sheets halfway through baking. Allow to cool upside-down.

4. Combine lettuce, tomatoes, scallions, and two tablespoons cilantro in a large bowl; toss with lime juice and season with sea salt and pepper to taste. Place Tortilla bowls on individual plates. Divide salad among bowls, top with taco meat, and sprinkle with remaining two tablespoons cilantro. Serve.

Tortillas

MAKES 5-6 TORTILLAS

Ingredients

3 large eggs

4 egg whites (⅔ cup)

½ to ¾ cup water (start with ½ cup, adding more as necessary to achieve desired thinness)

1 tablespoon melted lard (cooled) or coconut oil

1 cup tapioca starch/flour

½ teaspoon almond meal (almonds ground to meal using a food processor; not quite as finely ground as almond flour)

2 tablespoons coconut flour

½ teaspoon baking powder

½ teaspoon sea salt

Lard or coconut oil for grilling tortillas

Preparation

1. Whisk the eggs, egg whites, and water in a bowl. Still whisking, drizzle in one tablespoon of melted lard or coconut oil.

2. In a separate bowl, whisk the tapioca starch/flour, almond meal, coconut flour, baking powder, and sea salt together to combine.

3. Mix the dry ingredients into the wet ingredients, whisking until well combined and smooth. The batter will be very thin.

4. Heat a crepe pan or flat-bottomed, nonstick skillet or grill pan over medium-high heat. Add lard or coconut oil and heat until shimmering.

5. Pour about ⅓ cup of the batter on the hot pan surface. Holding onto the handle of the pan, remove it from the heat and quickly swirl the pan so the batter coats the bottom and you have an approximately eight-inch Tortilla.

6. Grill for 1 to 2 minutes on one side, then flip and grill for 30 seconds to 1 minute on the other (don't overcook, or they will not stay pliable).

Cheeseburgers with Lettuce Wraps

SERVES 4

Ingredients

---

1 slice White Sandwich Bread, chopped (see page 19)

2 tablespoons coconut milk

4 ounces ground turkey breast

2 teaspoons Worcestershire Sauce (see page 230)

¼ teaspoon sea salt

½ teaspoon pepper

12 ounces ground beef

1 teaspoon coconut oil or Rendered Animal Fat (see page ix)

4 slices Coconut Milk Cheddar Cheese (see page 239)

4 large lettuce leave or 4 slices White Sandwich Bread (see page 19)

Preparation

1. Mash 1 slice bread and milk together in large bowl with fork until combined. Add ground turkey, Worcestershire Sauce, sea salt, and pepper and mix until smooth.

2. Break up ground beef into small pieces and sprinkle over turkey and bread mixture. Using hands, gently combine meats until smooth. Divide meat into four equal portions. Working with one portion of meat at a time, toss meat back and forth between hands to form a loose ball, then gently flatten into half-inch-thick patty, about four to five inches wide.

3. Heat oil in twelve-inch nonstick skillet over medium heat until just smoking. Lay patties in skillet, cover, and cook, without moving them, until well-browned, about 3 minutes. Flip burgers, cover, and continue to cook 2 minutes longer. Top each burger with one slice of cheese, cover, and continue to cook until cheese is melted and burgers register 160° F, about 1 minute. Transfer burgers to lettuce leaves or sandwich bread and serve.

Chef's Note: If you'd like a little more flavor on your burger, add tomatoes, Lacto-Fermented vegetables, Mustard, Ketchup, Mayonnaise (see page 214), or anything else that sounds appealing.

Sloppy Joes

SERVES 4

Ingredients

6 ounces white mushrooms, trimmed and sliced thin

2 teaspoons coconut oil or Rendered Animal Fat (see page ix)

Sea salt and pepper to taste

1 onion, chopped fine

1¼ teaspoons chili powder

1 (8-ounce) can tomato sauce

¼ cup Ketchup (see page 221)

¼ cup water

1 tablespoon Worcestershire Sauce (see page 230)

1 teaspoon packed brown sugar

1 teaspoon balsamic vinegar

10 ounces ground beef

4 large lettuce leaves or White Sandwich Bread (see page 19)

Preparation

1. Combine mushrooms, one teaspoon oil, and ¼ teaspoon sea salt in twelve-inch nonstick skillet. Cover and cook over medium-low heat until softened, 8 to 10 minutes. Uncover, increase heat to medium-high, and cook, stirring occasionally, until mushrooms are well browned, 8 to 12 minutes. Transfer mushrooms to food processor and pulse until finely ground, about six pulses.

2. Heat remaining teaspoon of oil in the now-empty skillet over medium heat until shimmering. Add processed mushrooms and onion, cover, and cook until onion is softened, 8 to 12 minutes. Stir in chili powder and cook until fragrant, about 30 seconds. Add tomato sauce, Ketchup, water, Worcestershire Sauce, sugar, and vinegar. Bring to a simmer, then reduce heat to medium-low and cook until slightly thickened, about 15 minutes.

3. Stir in ground beef, breaking up meat with a wooden spoon, and simmer until no longer pink, about 5 minutes. Season with sea salt and pepper to taste. Divide meat mixture among lettuce leaves or sandwich bread and serve.

Reuben Sandwiches

SERVES 4

Ingredients

½ cup Mayonnaise (see page 214)

¼ cup relish of Lacto-Fermented cucumbers (see page 218)

3 tablespoons Ketchup (see page 221)

1 tablespoon lemon juice

1 garlic clove, minced

¼ teaspoon sea salt

¼ teaspoon pepper

8 slices Hearty Sandwich Bread (see page 20)

6 ounces Coconut Milk Cheddar Cheese, shredded (optional; see page 239)

1⅓ cups Lacto-Fermented sauerkraut, rinsed, drained, and squeezed dry (see page 218)

1 pound Cured Corned Beef, thinly sliced (page 40)

Preparation

1. Adjust oven racks to the middle and lower-middle positions and preheat oven to 450° F. Place one baking sheet on each rack. Mix Mayonnaise, relish, Ketchup, lemon juice, garlic, sea salt, and pepper together in a bowl.

2. Spread one tablespoon Mayonnaise mixture onto one side of each bread slice. Assemble four sandwiches by layering the following ingredients on four slices of bread, with Mayonnaise mixture inside: half of cheese, sauerkraut, remaining Mayonnaise mixture, corned beef, and remaining cheese. Top with remaining four slices of bread and press gently on sandwiches to compact.

3. Carefully lay sandwiches on the hot sheet on the middle rack, then top with the second hot sheet. Bake sandwiches until heated through and bread is toasted, 12 to 15 minutes. Serve warm.

Cured Corned Beef

Ingredients

Pickling Spices*

1 tablespoon whole allspice berries

1 tablespoon whole mustard seeds (brown or yellow)

1 tablespoon coriander seeds

1 tablespoon red pepper flakes

1 tablespoon whole cloves

1 tablespoon whole black peppercorns

9 whole cardamom pods

6 large bay leaves, crumbled

2 teaspoons ground ginger

½ stick cinnamon

Brine

1 gallon water

2 cups sea salt

5 teaspoons pink curing sea salt**

4 tablespoons pickling spices, divided

½ cup brown sugar

1 five-pound beef brisket

* The spiced gallon of brine easily makes enough curing brine for a five-pound brisket in a large rigid container. If using a two-gallon freezer bag or a marinating bag, reduce the brine ingredients by half.

** Pink curing salt, or sodium nitrite, has multiple names, such as Prague Powder #1 or DQ Curing Salt #1. It's available for purchase online and may be available at your local specialty market or butcher shop. If you aren't able to obtain it, you can still make cured corned beef, but it is necessary for that vibrant pink color we associate with corned beef. It adds flavor as well. Without it, the corned beef will be a dull gray color. Paleo purists will not use the pink curing salt. I've cured corned beef both ways, and it's purely a matter of taste and aesthetics.

Preparation

1. You may use either store-bought pickling spices or you can prepare your own using the recipe provided. To prepare the recipe, toast the allspice berries, mustard seeds, coriander seeds, red pepper flakes, cloves, peppercorns, and cardamom pods in a small frying pan on high heat until fragrant and you hear the mustard seeds start to pop.

2. Remove the frying pan from the heat and place the toasted spices in a mortar. Use a pestle to roughly crush the spices. Add the crushed spices to a small bowl and stir in the crumbled bay leaves and ground ginger.

3. Add three tablespoons of the spice mixture (reserve the rest for cooking the corned beef after it has cured), plus the ½ stick of cinnamon, to a gallon of water in a large pot, along with the sea salt, pink sea salt (if using), and brown sugar. Bring to a boil, then remove from heat and allow to cool to room temperature. Refrigerate until well chilled.

4. Place the chilled brisket in a large, flat container or pan and cover with the brine. If the meat floats, weigh it down with a plate. Alternatively, you can use a two-gallon freezer bag (placed in a container so that if it leaks, it doesn't leak all over your refrigerator). Place the brisket in the freezer bag with about two quarts of brine, squeezing the air out of the bag before sealing. Place the meat in the refrigerator and chill for five to seven days. Flip the brisket over each day so that all sides are brined equally.

5. At the end of five days, remove the brisket from the brine and rinse with cold water to remove the brine. Place the brisket in a large pot that just fits around the brisket and cover with at least one inch of water. If you want your brisket to taste less salty, add another inch of water to the pot. Add one tablespoon of the pickling spices to the pot. Bring to a boil, reduce to low, and simmer for three to four hours, until the corned beef is fork tender. Or pressure cook on high for 70 minutes and quick depressurization.

6. Remove the meat to a cutting board. Slice thinly against the grain and serve warm. Store in an airtight container in the refrigerator for up to seven days. Use the refrigerated corned beef on your favorite sandwich. The Reuben Sandwich recipe is the perfect use for this home-cured corned beef.

Chef's Note: You may reserve the liquid used to cook the corned beef for cooking vegetables to serve with the beef. Potatoes and cabbage are a traditional Irish dish that is often cooked in the corned beef liquid and served with a couple of slices of corned beef.

French Onion Soup

Ingredients

Sea salt and pepper to taste

Coconut oil or Rendered Beef Tallow, for greasing Dutch oven (see page ix)

4 pounds yellow onions, halved and sliced ¼-inch thick

3 cups water, plus extra as needed for cooking the onions

½ cup dry sherry

4 cups Chicken Broth or Stock (see page 236)

2 cups Beef Broth or Stock (see page 236)

6 sprigs fresh thyme, tied with kitchen twine

1 bay leaf

6 slices of White Sandwich Bread (see page 19)

Preparation

1. Adjust oven rack to the lower-middle position and preheat oven to 400° F. Grease inside of a Dutch oven with oil or fat, then stir in onions and ½ teaspoon sea salt. Cover, transfer pot to oven, and cook for one hour (onions will be moist and slightly reduced in volume).

2. Stir onions thoroughly, scraping bottom and sides of pot. Partially cover pot and continue to cook in oven until onions are a deep golden brown, one hour and 30 to 45 minutes longer, stirring onions and scraping bottom and sides of pot every 30 minutes.

3. Remove pot from oven and place over medium-high heat. Cook, stirring onions and scraping bottom and sides of pot often, until liquid evaporates and pot is coated with a dark crust, 20 to 28 minutes; reduce heat if onions brown too quickly.

4. Stir in ¼ cup water and scrape pot bottom to loosen crust. Cook until water evaporates and another dark crust has formed on pot bottom, 6 to 8 minutes. Repeat two or three more times, adding more water as necessary, until onions are very dark brown.

5. Stir in sherry and cook, stirring often, until evaporated, about 5 minutes. Stir in remaining two cups water, Chicken Broth or Stock, Beef Broth or Stock, thyme, and bay leaf. Bring to simmer, cover, and cook for 30 minutes. Remove thyme and bay leaf. Season soup with sea salt and pepper to taste.

6. Meanwhile, arrange bread in single layer on baking sheet. Bake until edges are golden, about 10 minutes; set aside.

7. Fill individual crocks with soup. Top with toasted bread slices and serve immediately.

Chef's Note: If you want the traditional version of this soup, position oven rack six inches from the broiling element and turn on the broiler. Be sure to use broiler proof crocks for the soup. Add a slice of Coconut Milk Cheddar Cheese (see page 239) on top of the toasted bread, place individual crocks on a rimmed baking sheet and place in the oven. Broil until cheese is bubbly and slightly browned, one to two minutes. Remove from oven and cool for 2 minutes. Serve warm.

Creamy Tomato Soup

Ingredients

¼ cup coconut oil or Rendered Animal Fat (see page ix)

1 onion, chopped fine

3 garlic cloves, minced

1 bay leaf

Pinch red pepper flakes

2 (28-ounce) cans whole peeled tomatoes

1 tablespoon palm sugar

3 slices White Sandwich Bread, crusts removed, torn into 1-inch pieces (see page 19)

2 cups Chicken Broth or Stock (see page 236)

2 tablespoons brandy

Sea salt and pepper to taste

¼ cup minced fresh chives

Preparation

1. Heat two tablespoons oil in Dutch oven over medium heat until shimmering. Add onion and cook until softened, 5 to 7 minutes. Stir in garlic, bay leaf, and pepper flakes and cook until fragrant, about 30 seconds.

2. Stir in tomatoes and their juices. Using a potato masher, mash until no pieces larger than two inches wide remain. Stir in sugar and bread and bring to a simmer. Reduce heat to medium and cook, stirring occasionally, until bread is completely saturated and starts to break down, about 5 minutes. Remove bay leaf.

3. Working in batches, process soup with remaining two tablespoons oil in blender until smooth. Return soup to clean pot and stir in Chicken Broth or Stock and brandy. Reheat soup gently over medium-low heat. Season with sea salt and pepper to taste. Garnish individual bowls with chives before serving.

Creamy Mushroom Soup

SERVES 6

Ingredients

1 tablespoon coconut oil or Rendered Animal Fat (see page ix)

2 pounds white mushrooms, trimmed and quartered

1 pound leeks, white and light green parts only, halved lengthwise, sliced thin, and washed thoroughly

Sea salt and pepper to taste

4 garlic cloves, minced

2 teaspoons minced fresh thyme or ½ teaspoon dried thyme

5 cups Beef Broth or Stock (see page 236)

½ cup Madeira, plus extra for serving

½ cup coconut milk

2 teaspoons lemon juice, freshly squeezed

Preparation

1. Melt fat in a Dutch oven over medium-low heat. Add mushrooms, leeks, ½ teaspoon sea salt, and ¼ teaspoon pepper, cover, and cook until mushrooms are softened and wet, 8 to 10 minutes. Uncover, increase heat to medium-high, and cook, stirring occasionally, until mushrooms are dry and well browned, 8 to 12 minutes. Transfer ⅔ cup of mushroom mixture to cutting board and chop fine; set aside.

2. Stir garlic and thyme into pot and cook until fragrant, about 30 seconds. Stir in broth and Madeira, bring to a simmer, and cook until mushrooms and leeks are completely tender, about 20 minutes. Cool before proceeding to next step.

3. Working in batches, process soup in blender until smooth. Return soup to clean pot and stir in chopped mushroom mixture, coconut milk, and lemon juice. Reheat soup gently over medium-low heat and season with sea salt and pepper to taste. Drizzle individual bowls with extra Madeira before serving.

New England Clam Chowder

SERVES 6

Ingredients

2 slices bacon, chopped fine

1 onion, chopped fine

2 garlic cloves, minced

¼ teaspoon dried thyme

1 pound turnips, peeled and cut into ½-inch chunks

¼ cup dry white wine

2 bay leaves

4 (6.5-ounce) cans chopped clams, drained, juice reserved

1 tablespoon tapioca or arrowroot starch

1 (8-ounce) bottle paleo-friendly clam juice

¾ cup coconut milk

1 tablespoon minced fresh parsley

Sea salt and pepper to taste

Preparation

1. Cook bacon in a Dutch oven over medium heat until rendered and crisp, about 3 minutes. Stir in onion and cook until softened, 5 to 7 minutes. Stir in garlic and thyme and cook until fragrant, about 30 seconds. Stir in turnips, wine, bay leaves, and reserved clam juice. Bring to a simmer and cook until turnips are tender, 10 to 12 minutes.

2. Whisk tapioca or arrowroot starch and bottled clam juice together in a bowl, then add to the pot and simmer until thickened. Stir in coconut milk, parsley, and chopped clams and simmer gently until clams are heated through, about 2 minutes; do not boil. Remove bay leaves and season with sea salt and pepper to taste. Serve.

Shrimp Bisque

SERVES 7

Ingredients

2 pounds medium shrimp, wild-caught

⅓ cup brandy or cognac

1 onion, chopped coarse

1 carrot, peeled and chopped coarse

1 celery rib, chopped coarse

1 garlic clove, peeled

⅓ cup tapioca or arrowroot flour

1 cup dry white wine

4 (8-ounce) bottles paleo-friendly
    clam juice

1 (14.5-ounce) can diced
    tomatoes, drained

1 cup coconut milk

1 tablespoon lemon juice,
    fresh squeezed

1 sprig fresh tarragon

Rendered Animal Fat (see page ix)

Sea salt and pepper to taste

2 tablespoons minced fresh chives

Preparation

1. Peel and devein one pound of shrimp, reserving shells, and cut each shrimp into three pieces; refrigerate until needed.

2. Heat a twelve-inch skillet over medium-high heat until just smoking. Add remaining pound of shrimp and reserved shrimp shells and cook until lightly browned, about 5 minutes. Remove from heat, add brandy, and warm through, about 5 seconds. Wave a lit match over the pan until brandy ignites, then shake pan to distribute flames.

3. When flames subside, transfer flambéed shrimp mixture to a food processor and process until the mixture resembles a fine meal, 10 to 20 seconds. Transfer to bowl. Pulse onion, carrot, celery, and garlic in food processor until finely chopped, about five pulses.

4. Combine processed shrimp and vegetables in a Dutch oven. Cover and cook over medium-low heat, stirring occasionally, until softened and fragrant, 5 to 7 minutes. Stir in flour and cook for an additional minute. Gradually whisk in wine and clam juice, scraping up any browned bits and smoothing out any lumps. Stir in tomatoes, bring to a simmer, and cook until thickened and flavors meld, about 20 minutes.

5. Strain broth through a fine-mesh strainer, pressing on solids to release as much liquid as possible. Discard solids and wipe pot clean.

6. Combine strained broth, coconut milk, lemon juice, and tarragon in the now-empty pot and bring to a simmer. Stir in reserved shrimp pieces and simmer until shrimp are bright pink, 1 to 2 minutes. Remove from heat, discard tarragon, stir in oil or Rendered Animal Fat, and season with sea salt and pepper to taste. Sprinkle individual portions with chives before serving.

Chef's Note: Shrimp come in a variety of sizes and are typically identified by count per pound. Use this chart determine which shrimp to purchase for the recipe. Shrimp per pound:

- 10 shrimp or less = Colossal
- 11 to 15 = Jumbo
- 16 to 20 = Extra-large
- 21 to 30 = Large
- 31 to 35 = Medium
- 36 to 45 = Small
- about 100 = Miniature

All-American Chili

Ingredients

Sea salt and pepper to taste

1 tablespoon coconut oil or Rendered Animal Fat (see page ix)

2 onions, chopped fine

1 red bell pepper, stemmed, seeded, and cut into ½-inch pieces

6 garlic cloves, minced

¼ cup chili powder

1 tablespoon ground cumin

2 teaspoons ground coriander

1 teaspoon red pepper flakes

1 teaspoon dried oregano

½ teaspoon cayenne pepper

30 ounces ground beef

2 pounds ground turkey

2 (15-ounce) cans kidney beans, rinsed

1 (28-ounce) can diced tomatoes

1 (28-ounce) can crushed tomatoes

2 cups Chicken Broth or Stock (see page 236)

Preparation

1. Heat oil in a Dutch oven over medium heat until shimmering. Add onions, bell pepper, garlic, chili powder, cumin, coriander, pepper flakes, oregano, and cayenne to Dutch oven and cook, stirring often, until vegetables are softened, 8 to 10 minutes.

2. Add one pound of turkey and the ground beef to the Dutch oven, increase heat to medium-high, and cook, breaking up the meat with a wooden spoon, until no longer pink and just beginning to brown, about 4 minutes. Stir in beans, diced tomatoes and their juices, crushed tomatoes, and broth and bring to a simmer. Reduce heat to medium-low and simmer until chili has begun to thicken, about one hour.

3. Pat the remaining pound of turkey together into a ball, then pinch off teaspoon-sized pieces and stir into chili. Continue to simmer, stirring occasionally, until turkey is tender and chili is slightly thickened, about 40 minutes longer. (If chili begins to stick to bottom of pot, stir in ½ cup water.) Season with sea salt and pepper to taste. Serve.

Beef and Vegetable Stew

Serves 6

Ingredients

2 pounds boneless beef chuck-eye roast, trimmed of all visible fat, and cut into 1½-inch pieces

Sea salt and pepper to taste

5 teaspoons coconut oil or Rendered Animal Fat (see page ix)

1 large portobello mushroom cap, cut into ½-inch pieces

2 onions, chopped fine

3 garlic cloves, minced

1 tablespoon minced fresh thyme or 1 teaspoon dried thyme

3 tablespoons tapioca or arrowroot flour

1 tablespoon tomato paste

1½ cups dry red wine

2 cups Chicken Broth or Stock (see page 236)

2 cups Beef Broth or Stock (see page 236)

2 bay leaves

4 carrots, peeled, halved lengthwise, and

sliced 1 inch thick

4 turnips, peeled, halved lengthwise, and sliced 1 inch thick

1 pound kale, stemmed and sliced into ½-inch-wide strips

¼ cup minced fresh parsley (sprinkling)

Preparation

1. Adjust oven rack to lower-middle position and preheat oven to 300° F. Pat beef dry with paper towels and season with sea salt and pepper. Heat one teaspoon of oil or fat in a Dutch oven over medium-high heat until shimmering. Brown half of meat on all sides, 5 to 10 minutes; transfer to a bowl. Repeat with an additional teaspoon oil or fat and remaining beef; transfer to bowl.

2. Add portobello pieces to oil or fat left in pot, cover, and cook over medium heat until softened and wet, about 5 minutes. Uncover and continue to cook until portobello pieces are dry and browned, 5 to 10 minutes.

3. Stir in remaining tablespoon of oil or fat and onions and cook until softened, about 5 to 7 minutes. Stir in garlic and thyme and cook until fragrant, about 30 seconds. Stir in flour and tomato paste and cook until lightly browned, about 1 minute.

4. Slowly whisk in wine, scraping up any browned bits. Slowly whisk in broths until smooth. Stir in bay leaves and browned meat and bring to a simmer. Cover, transfer pot to oven, and cook for an hour and a half.

5. Stir in turnips and carrots, and continue to cook in oven until meat and vegetables are tender, about one hour. Stir in kale and continue to cook in oven until tender, about 10 minutes. Remove stew from oven and discard bay leaves. Stir in parsley and allow stew to sit for 5 to 10 minutes. Season with sea salt and pepper to taste. Serve.

{ Vegetable Sides }

Spaghetti Squash

SERVES 6-8

Ingredients

2-3 pounds spaghetti squash
Water for baking squash

Preparation

1. Preheat oven to 350° F and place an oven rack in the center position. Carefully cut the spaghetti squash in half using a sharp chef's knife or cleaver.
2. Using a spoon, scrape out seeds from the center of both halves of the squash.
3. Pour two inches of water into a rimmed baking sheet and place each half of the squash, cut side down, in the water. Place the baking sheet in the oven and bake for 45 minutes.
4. Remove the squash from the oven and allow it to cool enough to handle. Using a fork, pull the squash away from the outer shell. The squash will separate easily into spaghetti-like strands.
5. Set squash aside and keep warm until serving with favorite sauce or topping. Squash will keep for up to three days in the refrigerator in an airtight container.

Broccoli with Cheese Sauce

Ingredients

1½ pounds broccoli florets, cut into 1-inch pieces

Coconut oil, melted

1 cup Chicken Broth or Stock (see page 236)

Pinch cayenne pepper

1 tablespoon tapioca or arrowroot starch

½ teaspoon Dijon Mustard (see page 225)

4 ounces Coconut Milk Cheddar Cheese (see page 239)

Hot water

Sea salt and pepper to taste

Preparation

1. Adjust oven rack to lower-middle position, place rimmed baking sheet on rack, and preheat oven to 450° F. Toss broccoli lightly with oil, then arrange in a single layer on preheated baking sheet. Roast until spotty brown, 15 to 18 minutes, stirring halfway through roasting time.

2. Meanwhile, combine ¾ cup broth and cayenne in a small saucepan and bring to a simmer. Whisk remaining ¼ cup broth, tapioca or arrowroot starch, and Dijon Mustard together, then whisk into simmering broth. Bring to a boil, whisking constantly, until sauce is slightly thickened, about 2 minutes. Turn heat to low and whisk in cheese until melted and smooth. (If sauce becomes too thick, stir in hot water, one tablespoon at a time, to thin to desired consistency.) Season with sea salt and pepper to taste. Transfer broccoli to a large platter, pour sauce over top, and serve.

Creamed Spinach

SERVES 4

Ingredients

¼ cup water

3 (10-ounce) bags curly-leaf spinach, stemmed and chopped coarse

¼ cup coconut milk

4 ounces (½ cup) Boursin Cheese (optional; see page 240)

Sea salt and pepper

Preparation

1. Add water to Dutch oven and place over medium-high heat. Stir in spinach, a handful at a time, and cook until fully wilted, glossy, and tender, 30 seconds to 1 minute. Transfer spinach to a colander and squeeze with tongs or press firmly with the back of a large spoon to remove excess liquid.

2. Wipe the now-empty pot dry with paper towels and add coconut milk. Whisk in Boursin and simmer over medium heat until slightly thickened, about 1 minute. Remove from heat and stir in drained spinach until evenly coated with sauce. Season with sea salt and pepper to taste. Serve.

Cheesy Cauliflower Bake

SERVES 10

Ingredients

Coconut oil for greasing baking dish

3 slices White Sandwich Bread, torn into pieces (see page 19)

2 teaspoons olive oil

6 ounces Coconut Milk Cheddar Cheese, shredded (see page 239)

3 garlic cloves, minced

Sea salt and pepper to taste

1¼ cups coconut milk

¾ cup Chicken Broth or Stock (see page 236)

2 teaspoons dry mustard powder

1 teaspoon minced fresh thyme

2 heads cauliflower (4 pounds), cored and cut into ¾-inch florets

1 tablespoon tapioca or arrowroot starch

1 tablespoon water

Preparation

1. Adjust oven rack to middle position and preheat oven to 450° F. Grease a 13x9-inch baking dish with coconut oil. Pulse bread in a food processor to create coarse crumbs, about 10 pulses. Toast breadcrumbs in oil in a twelve-inch nonstick skillet over medium heat, stirring often, until well browned, about 10 minutes; allow to cool. Combine cooled crumbs, two tablespoons cheddar, one teaspoon garlic, ¼ teaspoon sea salt, and ¼ teaspoon pepper in bowl.

2. Whisk remaining garlic, coconut milk, broth, mustard powder, thyme, ¼ teaspoon sea salt, and ¼ teaspoon pepper together in Dutch oven. Add cauliflower and bring to a simmer over medium-high heat. Reduce heat to low, partially cover, and simmer, stirring occasionally, until cauliflower is nearly tender, 5 to 7 minutes.

3. Whisk tapioca or arrowroot starch and water together in bowl, then add to pot, bring to a simmer, and cook, stirring constantly, until sauce has thickened slightly. Remove from heat and stir in remaining cheddar until fully incorporated.

4. Pour cauliflower mixture into prepared baking dish and top evenly with toasted crumb mixture. Bake until bubbling around edges and crumbs are crisp, 8 to 12 minutes. Allow to cool for 10 minutes before serving.

Mashed Turnips

SERVES 6

Ingredients

2 pounds turnips, peeled and sliced ½-inch thick

 Sea salt and pepper to taste

⅔ cup coconut milk, room temperature

¼ teaspoon lemon juice, freshly squeezed

3 tablespoons olive oil

Preparation

1. Place turnips and one tablespoon sea salt in a large saucepan and add water to cover turnips by one inch. Bring to a boil over high heat, then reduce to medium-low and simmer gently until turnips are tender but not falling apart, 15 to 18 minutes.

2. Drain turnips, then return to saucepan on still-warm stovetop. Using a potato masher, mash turnips until smooth. Gently stir milk, lemon juice, and olive oil together in a bowl until combined. Gently fold milk mixture into turnips until just incorporated. Season with sea salt and pepper to taste and serve.

Twice-Baked Sweet Potato Casserole

SERVES 8

Ingredients

4 (8-ounce) sweet potatoes (orange, purple, or Japanese), unpeeled

1 teaspoon coconut oil

½ cup crushed pineapple, fresh, unsweetened

½ teaspoon cinnamon, ground (to taste, plus extra for sprinkling)

4 tablespoons coconut milk

Pinch of sea salt

¼ cup palm sugar

Preparation

1. Grease an eight-inch square baking dish with coconut oil. Adjust oven racks to upper-middle and middle positions and preheat oven to 400° F. Rub sweet potatoes with oil, place directly on upper oven rack, and bake until skins are crisp and deep brown and a skewer glides easily through the flesh, about one hour, flipping them over halfway through baking.

2. Line a rimmed baking sheet with aluminum foil; top with wire rack. Transfer baked sweet potatoes to rack; allow to cool slightly, about 10 minutes. Increase oven temperature to 500° F.

3. Cut each potato in half lengthwise, through the narrow side, so that halved potatoes lie flat. Carefully scoop the flesh from each potato half into a medium bowl. Discard the potato skins. Mash potato flesh with a potato masher or fork until smooth, then stir in pineapple, cinnamon, and one pinch of sea salt. Spoon mixture into prepared baking dish, mounding it slightly at center. Sprinkle with cinnamon and palm sugar.

4. Bake mashed sweet potatoes on middle rack until heated through, 10 to 15 minutes.

Chef's Note: For a more traditional version of this recipe, remove the sweet potato from the skins being careful not to tear the skins. Reserve the skins and refill with the potato mixture in step 3. Place stuffed potato skins on a coconut oil greased rimmed baking sheet and proceed with step 4, reducing the baking time to 7-10 minutes.

Scalloped Turnips or Rutabagas

SERVES 6

Ingredients

Coconut oil for greasing baking dish

1½ teaspoons coconut oil

1 onion, minced

Sea salt and pepper to taste

1 garlic clove, minced

1 teaspoon minced fresh thyme

2½ pounds turnips or rutabagas, peeled and sliced ⅛-inch thick

2 cups coconut milk

2 bay leaves

2 teaspoons tapioca or arrowroot starch

1 tablespoon water

3 tablespoons coconut milk

2 ounces Coconut Milk Cheddar Cheese, grated (see page 239)

Preparation

1. Adjust oven rack to middle position and preheat oven to 450° F. Grease an eight-inch baking dish with coconut oil. Heat oil in a Dutch oven over medium heat until shimmering. Add onion and ½ teaspoon sea salt and cook until softened, 5 to 7 minutes. Stir in garlic and thyme and cook until fragrant, about 30 seconds.

2. Add turnips or rutabagas, milk, and bay leaves and bring to a simmer. Cover, reduce heat to low, and simmer until partially tender (tip of a paring knife can be slipped into center of turnips or rutabagas with some resistance), about 10 minutes.

3. Remove bay leaves. Whisk tapioca or arrowroot starch and water together in bowl, then add to pot and bring to simmer. Remove from heat, stir in three tablespoons coconut milk, two tablespoons cheese, and ¼ teaspoon pepper, being careful not to break up turnips or rutabagas. Transfer mixture to prepared baking dish.

4. Sprinkle with remaining cheese. Cover dish with aluminum foil and bake until bubbling around edges, about 20 minutes. Remove foil and continue to bake until turnips or rutabagas are completely tender and top is golden brown, 10 to 15 minutes. Allow to cool for 10 minutes before serving.

Sweet Potato Casserole

Ingredients

---

3 tablespoons coconut oil

3¾ pounds sweet potatoes,(orange, purple, or Japanese) peeled, quartered, and cut crosswise into 1-inch pieces

½ cup palm sugar

1 teaspoon sea salt

¼ teaspoon pepper, black or red

½ cup water

2 cups Marshmallows (see page 241)

Preparation

1. Melt coconut oil in a Dutch oven over medium-high heat. Stir in sweet potatoes, sugar, sea salt, pepper, and water and bring to simmer. Cover, reduce heat to medium-low, and cook, stirring often, until sweet potatoes are completely tender, 35 to 45 minutes. Remove from heat and mash sweet potato mixture with a potato masher until smooth.

2. Adjust oven rack to a position six inches from the broiler element and heat broiler. Transfer potato mixture to a 13x9-inch broiler-safe casserole dish and top with marshmallows. Broil until marshmallows are slightly melted and golden, 3 to 4 minutes. Serve.

Caution: Watch your casserole closely while broiling. Many a marshmallow has gone up in flames under a broiler! If it catches on fire, place a cookie sheet over it to smother the flame. Then scrape off the burned marshmallows, add a new layer, and broil again.

Eggplant Gratin

SERVES 6

Ingredients

4½ teaspoons coconut oil, divided

1 small onion, diced

2 garlic cloves, minced

¼ teaspoon crushed red pepper

1 medium eggplant, peeled and cut into
 ½-inch cubes

1 medium tomato, chopped

2 tablespoons chopped fresh basil

½ teaspoon sea salt

½ cup fresh White Sandwich Breadcrumbs
 (see page 19)

1 ounce freshly grated Coconut Milk
 Cheddar Cheese (see page 239)

Preparation

1. Preheat the oven to 400°F. Grease a shallow 1½- to two-quart baking dish with ½ teaspoon of the oil.

2. Heat a small nonstick skillet over medium heat. Add two teaspoons of the remaining oil and tilt the pan to coat the bottom evenly. Add the onion and cook, stirring often, until softened, 5 minutes. Stir in the garlic and crushed red pepper and cook, stirring constantly, until fragrant, 30 seconds. Transfer to a large bowl

3. Meanwhile, in a pot fitted with a steamer basket, bring one inch of water to a boil over high heat. Add the eggplant cubes, reduce the heat to low, cover, and steam until they are tender but still retain their shape, about 5 minutes. Transfer to a colander to drain. Add to the bowl with the onion mixture. Stir in tomato, basil, and sea salt. Spoon eggplant into the prepared baking dish.

4. Stir together the breadcrumbs, cheese, and remaining two teaspoons of oil in a small bowl and sprinkle evenly over the eggplant mixture. Bake uncovered until the crumbs are brown, 20 to 25 minutes. Serve the gratin immediately.

Bacon Basil Mushrooms

SERVES 4

Ingredients

2 strips bacon, preferably uncured

1 small red onion, cut in half and sliced

2 garlic cloves, minced

1½ pounds cremini mushrooms, sliced

½ teaspoon sea salt

¼ teaspoon freshly ground pepper

3 tablespoons chopped fresh basil

Preparation

1. Cook the bacon in a large skillet over medium-high heat until crisp. Drain on paper towels and then chop. Pour off and discard all but two teaspoons of the drippings.

2. Add the onion to the bacon drippings and cook over medium-high heat, stirring often, until softened, about 5 minutes. Add the garlic and cook, stirring constantly, until fragrant, 30 seconds. Add the mushrooms and cook, stirring often, until the mushrooms are tender and most liquid has evaporated, about 8 minutes. Remove from heat and stir in the bacon and basil. Spoon the mushrooms into a serving dish and serve hot or warm.

Crispy Oven-Fried Onion Rings

SERVES 4

Ingredients

1 teaspoon plus 1 tablespoon coconut oil, divided
2 tablespoons tapioca or arrowroot flour
½ teaspoon sea salt
¼ teaspoon freshly ground pepper
⅛ teaspoon ground cayenne pepper
2 large eggs
2 tablespoons water
1 cup White Sandwich Breadcrumbs (see page 19)
2 large sweet onions

Preparation

1. Preheat the oven to 400° F. Line two large rimmed baking sheets with foil. Place a wire rack on each baking sheet and brush each rack with ½ teaspoon of the oil.
2. Combine the flour, sea salt, pepper, and cayenne in a large resealable plastic bag. Place the eggs and water in a shallow dish and beat lightly with a fork.
3. Combine the breadcrumbs with the remaining teaspoon of oil in another shallow dish using your fingers; blend the oil evenly into the crumbs.
4. Cut the onions into ½-inch thick slices and separate them into twenty-four large rings, reserving the smaller inner rings for another use. Place the onions, a few at a time, into the plastic bag. Shake bag to coat the onion rings. Dredge the onion rings in the egg mixture, then in the breadcrumbs, pressing to adhere the crumbs.
5. Arrange the onion rings in a single layer on the racks. Bake until onion rings are golden brown, 12 to 15 minutes. Do not turn. Serve immediately.

Oven-Fried Green Tomatoes

Ingredients

Coconut oil for greasing baking rack, melted

1 tablespoon olive oil

1 cup White Sandwich Breadcrumbs (see page 19)

1 ounce Coconut Milk Cheddar Cheese (see page 239)

¼ cup almond flour

2 egg whites, lightly beaten

2 medium green tomatoes, each cut into 4 ½-inch slices

1 teaspoon sea salt

⅛ teaspoon ground cayenne pepper

Preparation

1. Position an oven rack in the top third of the oven. Preheat oven to 400° F. Line a large rimmed baking sheet with foil. Place a wire rack in the baking sheet and brush the rack with ½ teaspoon of the coconut oil.

2. Place the breadcrumbs, cheese, and remaining tablespoon of oil in another shallow dish. Using your fingers, work the oil evenly into the crumb mixture. Place the almond flour in another shallow dish. Place the eggs in a third shallow dish.

3. Place the tomato slices in a large bowl and sprinkle with the sea salt and cayenne. Coat the tomato slices, one at a time, in the almond flour, then in the eggs, and finally in the breadcrumb mixture, pressing to adhere the crumbs.

4. Arrange the tomato slices in a single layer on the rack. Bake until golden brown, 30 to 35 minutes, and do not flip over. Serve at once.

Cauliflower "Mac" & Cheese

SERVES 4

Ingredients

Coconut oil for greasing baking dish

5 cups cauliflower florets

Sea salt and pepper to taste

1 cup coconut milk

½ cup Chicken Broth or Stock
  (see page 236)

½ cup tapioca flour

1 egg, beaten

2 cups Coconut Milk Cheddar
  Cheese, shredded
  (see page 239)

Preparation

1. Preheat the oven to 350° F. Grease a 9x13-inch baking dish with coconut oil.

2. Salt the cauliflower, then steam in a vegetable steamer until crisp and tender, 4 to 6 minutes.

3. Place the florets in prepared baking dish. Add tapioca flour to Chicken Broth or Stock in a medium bowl, stir with a fork, and set aside. Over medium heat in a skillet, add coconut milk and a pinch of sea salt and pepper to taste. Add Chicken Broth or Stock/tapioca flour mixture to milk and stir until it thickens. Remove the sauce from heat and cool slightly.

4. Crack egg into a bowl and whisk; set aside. Whisk a small amount of the warm sauce into the egg to temper. Add tempered egg to skillet and whisk. Place skillet back on the stove over medium heat and whisk constantly until warmed through.

5. Pour sauce from skillet over cauliflower in prepared baking dish.

6. Sprinkle cheese evenly over the top of the cauliflower and bake for 35 to 40 minutes until cheese is golden brown and bubbly. Remove from oven and serve warm. Sprinkle with additional cheese if desired before serving.

{ Poultry }

Oven-Fried Chicken

SERVES 4

Ingredients

Coconut oil for greasing baking rack

½ cup tapioca or arrowroot flour

4 large eggs

½ cup coconut milk

¼ teaspoon lemon juice

1½ teaspoons Dijon Mustard (see page 225)

3 cups almond flour

1 tablespoon coconut oil

¼ teaspoon garlic powder

 Sea salt and pepper

⅛ teaspoon poultry seasoning

Pinch cayenne pepper

4 (12-ounce) bone-in split chicken breasts, skin removed, trimmed of all visible fat, and halved

---

Preparation

1. Adjust oven rack to upper-middle position and preheat oven to 425° F. Line a rimmed baking sheet with aluminum foil, top with wire rack, and grease rack with oil. Spread flour into a shallow dish. In a second shallow dish, whisk eggs, then whisk in coconut milk, lemon juice, and Mustard. In a third shallow dish, combine almond flour, oil, garlic powder, ½ teaspoon sea salt, ¼ teaspoon pepper, poultry seasoning, and cayenne.

2. Pat chicken dry with paper towels and season with sea salt and pepper. Working with one piece at a time and coating top and sides only, dredge chicken in flour, dip in egg mixture, then coat with almond flour mixture, pressing gently to adhere; lay on prepared wire rack with uncoated side of chicken facing down.

3. Bake until crumbs are golden and chicken registers 160° F, about ⸍ minutes. Serve.

Crispy Chicken Nuggets

SERVES 4

Ingredients

Coconut oil for greasing wire rack

1½ pounds boneless, skinless chicken breasts, trimmed of all visible fat

2 tablespoons Worcestershire Sauce (see page 230)

2 teaspoons onion powder

½ teaspoon garlic powder

½ teaspoon sea salt

¼ teaspoon pepper

½ cup tapioca or arrowroot flour

3 large eggs

2 cups White Sandwich Breadcrumbs, toasted (see page 19)

1 tablespoon coconut oil

Preparation

1. Adjust oven rack to middle position and preheat oven to 475° F. Line a rimmed baking sheet with aluminum foil, top with wire rack, and grease rack with oil. Cut each breast diagonally into thirds. Slice largest piece crosswise into half-inch-thick pieces and slice two smaller pieces diagonally into half-inch-thick pieces; you should have about 48 nuggets total. Toss chicken with Worcestershire Sauce, onion powder, garlic powder, sea salt, and pepper in a bowl, cover, and refrigerate for 30 minutes.

2. Spread flour in a shallow dish. In a second shallow dish, whisk eggs. In a third shallow dish, combine toasted breadcrumbs and oil. Pat chicken dry with paper towels. Working in batches, dredge chicken in flour, dip in eggs, then coat with breadcrumb mixture, pressing gently to adhere; lay on prepared wire rack.

3. Bake until chicken registers 160° F, 10 to 12 minutes. Serve.

General Tso's Chicken

SERVES 4

Ingredients

Coconut oil for greasing baking rack

¼ cup tapioca or arrowroot flour

3 large eggs

5 cups almond flour

1½ pounds boneless, skinless chicken breasts, trimmed of all visible fat, cut into 1-inch pieces

1⅔ cups Chicken Broth or Stock (see page 236)

⅓ cup Soy Sauce (see page 233)

¼ cup Apricot Jam (see Fruit Jam recipe on page 213)

3 tablespoons Hoisin Sauce (see page 234)

2 tablespoons tapioca or arrowroot starch

2 teaspoons coconut oil

4 garlic cloves, minced

1 tablespoon grated fresh ginger

¼ teaspoon red pepper flakes

Preparation

1. Adjust oven rack to upper-middle position and preheat oven to 475° F. Line a rimmed baking sheet with aluminum foil, top with wire rack, and grease rack with oil. Spread flour in a shallow dish. Whisk eggs in a second shallow dish. Spread almond flour in a third shallow dish. Pat chicken dry with paper towels. Working in batches, dredge chicken in flour, dip in eggs, then coat with almond flour, pressing gently to adhere; lay on prepared wire rack.

2. Bake until chicken registers 160° F and coating is brown and crisp, 12 to 15 minutes.

3. Meanwhile, whisk Chicken Broth or Stock, Soy Sauce, Apricot Jam, Hoisin Sauce, and tapioca or arrowroot starch together in bowl. Heat oil in a twelve-inch skillet over medium heat until shimmering. Add garlic, ginger, and pepper flakes and cook until fragrant, about 1 minute. Whisk in Soy Sauce mixture, bring to a simmer, and cook until thickened. Remove from heat, cover, and keep warm.

4. When chicken is cooked, return sauce to a simmer over medium-low heat. Add to cooked chicken and toss to coat. Serve immediately.

Turkey Tacos

SERVES 4

Ingredients

1 teaspoon coconut oil

1 onion, chopped fine

2 tablespoons chili powder

3 garlic cloves, minced

1 teaspoon dried oregano

1 pound lean ground turkey

½ cup canned tomato sauce

½ cup Chicken Broth or Stock (see page 236)

2 teaspoons apple cider vinegar, naturally fermented

1 teaspoon palm sugar

 Sea salt and pepper to taste

8 Tortillas or iceberg lettuce leaves (see page 32)

2 cups fresh lettuce, chopped (optional)

Diced tomatoes (optional)

Preparation

1. Heat oil in a twelve-inch nonstick skillet over medium-high heat until shimmering. Add onion and cook until softened, about 5 minutes. Stir in chili powder, garlic, and oregano and cook until fragrant, about 30 seconds. Add ground turkey and cook, breaking up meat with a wooden spoon, until almost cooked through but still slightly pink, about 2 minutes.

2. Stir in tomato sauce, Chicken Broth or Stock, vinegar, and palm sugar. Bring to a simmer and cook until thickened, about 4 minutes. Season with sea salt and pepper to taste. Divide filling evenly among Tortillas or lettuce leaves and serve. Top with lettuce and tomato if desired.

Chicken and Dumplings

SERVES 4

Ingredients

Stew

3 pounds bone-in split chicken breasts, trimmed of all visible fat

Sea salt and pepper to taste

1½ teaspoons coconut oil

4 carrots, peeled and cut into ¾-inch pieces

2 onions, chopped fine

1 celery rib, minced

¼ cup dry sherry

6 cups Chicken Broth or Stock (see page 236)

¼ cup tapioca or arrowroot flour

1 teaspoon minced fresh thyme or ¼ tea-spoon dried thyme

¼ cup minced fresh parsley

Dumplings

2 cups (10 ounces) tapioca or arrowroot flour

⅓ cup coconut flour

1 teaspoon sea salt

½ teaspoon baking soda

¾ cup coconut milk

¼ teaspoon lemon juice, chilled

2 tablespoons coconut oil

1 large egg white

Preparation

1. **For the Stew:** Pat chicken dry with paper towels and season with sea salt and pepper. Heat oil in a large Dutch oven over medium-high heat until shimmering. Brown chicken well, 10 to 12 minutes; transfer to plate and remove skin.

2. Add carrots, onions, celery, and one teaspoon sea salt to fat left in pot, cover, and cook over medium-low heat, stirring occasionally, until softened, 8 to 10 minutes. Stir in sherry, scraping up any browned bits. Add broth, thyme, and chicken and any accumulated juices. Bring to a simmer, cover, and cook until chicken registers 160° F, about 20 minutes.

3. Remove pot from heat; transfer chicken to plate. When cool enough to handle, shred meat into large pieces, discarding the bones.

4. **For the Dumplings:** Whisk flours, sea salt, and baking soda together in a large bowl. In a separate bowl, stir chilled coconut milk, lemon juice, and melted coconut oil together. Whisk in the egg white. Add coconut milk mixture to flour mixture and stir with a fork

until just incorporated. Using a greased tablespoon, divide dough into equal portions. Shape individual portions into dumplings with greased hands. Set aside.

5. Return stew to a simmer and stir in shredded chicken and parsley. Season with sea salt and pepper to taste. Drop dumplings on top of stew, about one inch apart. Wrap lid of Dutch oven with clean kitchen towel (keeping towel away from heat source) and cover pot. Cook over low heat until dumplings are cooked through, 13 to 16 minutes. Serve.

Deviled Chicken

SERVES 4

Ingredients

3 tablespoons Mustard (see page 222)

2 tablespoons Mayonnaise (see page 214)

1½ tablespoons Louisiana-Style Fermented Hot Pepper Sauce (see page 226)

1 tablespoon lemon juice

3 garlic cloves, minced

½ teaspoon minced fresh thyme

Sea salt and pepper to taste

4 (6-ounce) boneless, skinless chicken breasts, trimmed of all visible fat

2 slices White Sandwich Bread, torn into pieces (see page 19)

1 tablespoon coconut oil

Preparation

1. Adjust oven rack to upper-middle position and preheat oven to 450° F. Combine Mustard, Mayonnaise, Louisiana-Style Fermented Hot Pepper Sauce, lemon juice, garlic, thyme, 1 tablespoon pepper, and ¾ teaspoon sea salt in large bowl. Stir in chicken, cover, and refrigerate for at least 30 minutes or up to three hours.

2. Meanwhile, pulse bread, ¼ teaspoon sea salt, and ¼ teaspoon pepper in food processor to form coarse crumbs, about 10 pulses. Melt coconut oil in a twelve-inch nonstick skillet over medium heat. Add crumbs and toast, stirring often, until golden, 5 to 7 minutes.

3. Line a rimmed baking sheet with aluminum foil, top with wire rack, and grease rack with coconut oil. Transfer marinated chicken to prepared wire rack. Sprinkle toasted breadcrumbs evenly over top, pressing gently to adhere. Bake until chicken registers 160° F, 20 to 25 minutes. Let chicken rest for 5 to 10 minutes before serving.

Nut-Crusted Chicken Breasts

SERVES 4

Ingredients

Coconut oil for greasing baking rack	1 tablespoon coconut oil
4 (6-ounce) boneless, skinless chicken breasts, trimmed of all visible fat	½ cup tapioca or arrowroot flour
	3 large eggs
Sea salt and pepper to taste	2 teaspoons Dijon Mustard (see page 225)
⅔ cup sliced almonds	1½ teaspoons grated lemon zest
⅔ cup White Sandwich Breadcrumbs (see page 19)	¾ teaspoon minced fresh thyme
	⅛ teaspoon cayenne pepper
1 shallot, minced	

Preparation

1. Adjust oven rack to lower-middle position and preheat oven to 350° F. Line a rimmed baking sheet with aluminum foil, top with wire rack, and grease rack with oil. Pat chicken dry with paper towels. Using a fork, poke the thicker half of each breast 5 to 6 times and sprinkle each with ¼ teaspoon sea salt. Transfer breasts to prepared wire rack and refrigerate, uncovered, while preparing coating.

2. Pulse almonds in a food processor until they resemble a coarse meal, about 20 pulses. Toast processed almonds, breadcrumbs, shallot in oil in a twelve-inch skillet over medium heat, stirring often, until golden brown, 8 to 10 minute; let cool.

3. Spread flour in a shallow dish. In a second shallow dish, whisk eggs and Dijon Mustard together until foamy. In a third shallow dish, combine toasted almond mixture, lemon zest, thyme, cayenne, ¼ teaspoon sea salt, and ¼ teaspoon pepper. Working with one piece of chicken at a time, dredge in flour, dip in egg mixture, then coat with nut mixture, pressing gently to adhere; return to wire rack.

4. Bake until chicken registers 160° F, 20 to 25 minutes. Let chicken rest for 5 to 10 minutes before serving..

Chicken Kiev

SERVES 4

Ingredients

Coconut oil for greasing baking rack

6 ounces Coconut Milk Cheddar Cheese, at room temperature (see page 239)

1 small shallot, minced

1 tablespoon minced fresh parsley

1 teaspoon lemon juice

½ teaspoon minced fresh tarragon

Sea salt and pepper to taste

4 (6-ounce) boneless, skinless chicken breasts, trimmed of all visible fat

½ cup tapioca or arrowroot flour

3 large eggs

1 teaspoon Dijon Mustard (see page 225)

⅔ cup White Sandwich Breadcrumbs, toasted (see page 19)

½ cup almond flour

1 tablespoon coconut oil

Preparation

1. Combine cheese, shallot, parsley, lemon juice, tarragon, ¼ teaspoon sea salt, and ¼ teaspoon pepper in bowl. Spread mixture into a three-inch square on a sheet of plastic wrap; wrap tightly and freeze until firm, at least one hour or up to four hours.

2. Using a chef's knife, butterfly each chicken breast by slicing it lengthwise almost in half. Open up breast to create a single, flat cutlet, then gently pound between sheets of plastic wrap to a quarter-inch thickness.. Season chicken with sea salt and pepper.

3. Cut chilled filling into four rectangles and place each on tapered end of cutlet. Roll bottom edge of chicken over filling, then fold in sides and continue to roll chicken up into a tidy package. Refrigerate, uncovered, to seal edges, about one hour.

4. Adjust oven rack to middle position and preheat oven to 350° F. Line a rimmed baking sheet with aluminum foil, top with wire rack, and grease rack with oil. Spread flour in a shallow dish. In a second shallow dish, whisk eggs and Dijon

Mustard together. In a third shallow dish, combine toasted breadcrumbs, almond flour, coconut oil, ¼ teaspoon sea salt, and ¼ teaspoon pepper.

5. Working with one piece of chicken at a time, dredge in flour, dip in egg mixture, then coat with breadcrumb mixture, pressing gently to adhere; lay on prepared wire rack. Spray chicken with oil spray. Bake until chicken registers 160° F, 40 to 45 minutes. Let chicken rest for 5 to 10 minutes before serving.

Chicken Fricassee

SERVES 4

Ingredients

4 (6-ounce) boneless, skinless chicken breasts, trimmed of all visible fat

Sea salt and pepper

2 teaspoons coconut oil

1 pound cremini mushrooms, trimmed and sliced ¼-inch thick

1 onion, chopped fine

¼ cup dry white wine

1 tablespoon tapioca or arrowroot flour

1 garlic clove, minced

1½ cups Chicken Broth or Stock (see page 236)

2 ounces Coconut Milk Cheddar Cheese, softened (see page 239)

2 teaspoons lemon juice

2 teaspoons minced fresh tarragon

¼ teaspoon ground nutmeg

Preparation

1. Pat chicken dry with paper towels and season with sea salt and pepper. Heat oil in a twelve-inch skillet over medium-high heat until just smoking. Brown chicken well on both sides, about 8 minutes total; transfer to plate.

2. Add mushrooms, onion, and wine to fat left in skillet and cook over medium heat until liquid has evaporated and mushrooms are browned, 8 to 10 minutes. Stir in garlic and cook for 1 minute. Slowly whisk in broth, scraping up any browned bits, and bring to boil. Return browned chicken and any accumulated juices to skillet. Reduce heat to medium-low, cover, and cook until chicken registers 160° F, about 10 minutes.

3. Transfer chicken to a serving platter and tent loosely with aluminum foil. Whisk ½ cup of sauce and tapioca flour into cheese in a bowl to temper, then stir cheese mixture back into pan. Stir in lemon juice, tarragon, and nutmeg and return sauce to a brief simmer. Season with sea salt and pepper to taste and pour over chicken. Serve.

Chicken Marsala

SERVES 4

Ingredients

½ cup tapioca or arrowroot flour

4 (6-ounce) boneless, skinless chicken breasts, trimmed of all visible fat

Sea salt and pepper

4 teaspoons coconut oil

8 ounces white mushrooms, trimmed and sliced thin

1 garlic clove, minced

2 teaspoons minced fresh thyme

1 cup Chicken Broth or Stock (see page 236)

½ cup Marsala wine

1 tablespoon water

1 teaspoon tapioca starch

1 tablespoon olive oil

Preparation

1. Spread flour in a shallow dish. Pat chicken dry with paper towels, season with sea salt and pepper, then lightly dredge in flour. Heat oil in a twelve-inch skillet over medium heat until shimmering. Add chicken and cook until golden on first side, 6 to 8 minutes. Flip chicken, reduce heat to medium-low, and continue to cook until chicken registers 160° F, 6 to 8 minutes; transfer to a platter and tent loosely with aluminum foil.

2. Add mushrooms and a pinch of sea salt to fat left in skillet, cover, and cook over medium heat until they have released their liquid, about 7 minutes. Uncover, increase heat to medium-high, and cook until mushrooms are well browned, about 7 minutes.

3. Stir in garlic and thyme and cook until fragrant, about 30 seconds. Whisk in broth and Marsala, scraping up any browned bits, and bring to a simmer. Whisk water and tapioca starch together in bowl, then stir into sauce and simmer until thickened. Remove from heat, whisk in olive oil, and season with sea salt and pepper to taste. Spoon sauce over chicken and serve.

Chicken Parmesan with Spaghetti Squash

SERVES 6

Ingredients

Coconut oil for greasing wire rack

½ cup tapioca or arrowroot flour

3 large eggs

½ teaspoon garlic powder

1½ cups White Sandwich Bread crumbs, toasted

1 tablespoon olive oil

Sea salt and pepper

6 (6-ounce) boneless, skinless chicken breasts, trimmed of all visible fat

12 ounces Spaghetti Squash, prepared (see page 59)

4 cups tomato sauce, warmed

4 ounces Coconut Milk Cheddar Cheese, shredded (see page 239)

1 tablespoon chopped fresh basil

Preparation

1. Adjust oven rack to middle position and preheat oven to 475° F. Line a rimmed baking sheet with aluminum foil, top with wire rack, and spray rack with oil spray. Spread flour in a shallow dish. In a second shallow dish, whisk eggs and garlic powder together. In a third shallow dish, combine toasted breadcrumbs, oil, ¼ teaspoon sea salt, and ¼ teaspoon pepper.

2. Place chicken between two sheets of plastic wrap and pound gently to an even half-inch thickness. Season chicken with sea salt and pepper. Working with one piece at a time, dredge chicken in flour, dip in egg mixture, then coat with bread crumb mixture, pressing gently to adhere; lay on prepared wire rack. Spray chicken with oil spray. Bake until chicken registers 160° F, 15 to 20 minutes.

3. In a pot, stir in prepared spaghetti squash with two cups tomato sauce. Season with sea salt and pepper to taste.

4. Top cutlets with one cup tomato sauce and sprinkle with cheese. Continue to bake until cheese has melted, 3 to 5 minutes. Sprinkle with basil and serve with squash mixture, passing remaining one cup tomato sauce separately.

Chicken Piccata with Spaghetti Squash

SERVES 4

Ingredients

¼ cup plus 1½ teaspoons tapioca or arrowroot flour

8 (3-ounce) boneless, skinless chicken breast cutlets, trimmed of all visible fat

Sea salt and pepper

5 teaspoons coconut oil

2 tablespoons capers, rinsed

2 garlic cloves, minced

1½ cups Chicken Broth or Stock (see page 236)

¾ cup dry white wine

4 (2-inch) strips lemon zest

4 teaspoons lemon juice

8 ounces Spaghetti Squash, prepared (see page 59)

1½ tablespoons olive oil

Preparation

1. Spread ¼ cup flour in a shallow dish. Pat cutlets dry with paper towels, season with sea salt and pepper, then lightly dredge one side of each cutlet in flour. Heat one tablespoon oil in a twelve-inch skillet over medium heat until shimmering. Add half of cutlets, floured side down, and cook until golden on first side, about 3 minutes. Flip cutlets and continue to cook until no longer pink, about 1 minute; transfer to a plate and tent loosely with aluminum foil. Repeat with remaining two teaspoons oil and remaining four cutlets.

2. Add capers and garlic to fat left in skillet and cook until fragrant, about 30 seconds. Stir in remaining 1½ teaspoons flour. Whisk in broth, wine, and lemon zest strips, scraping up any browned bits. Simmer sauce until slightly thickened and reduced to one cup, about 5 minutes.

3. In a pot, mix prepared spaghetti squash with ½ tablespoon olive oil and season with sea salt and pepper to taste; transfer to individual plates.

4. Return chicken cutlets and any accumulated juices to skillet and simmer until heated through, about 30 seconds. Arrange cutlets on top of pasta. Remove from heat, discard lemon zest, and whisk in lemon juice and remaining one tablespoon coconut oil. Spoon sauce over chicken and pasta and serve.

Chicken Cordon Bleu

SERVES 4

Ingredients

2 ounces Coconut Milk Cheddar Cheese, shredded (see page 239)

8 ounces ham

4 (8-ounce) boneless, skinless chicken breasts, trimmed of all visible fat

Coconut oil

½ cup tapioca or arrowroot flour

3 large eggs

2 tablespoons Dijon Mustard (see page 225)

⅔ cup White Sandwich Breadcrumbs, toasted (see page 19)

½ cup almond flour

1 tablespoon olive oil

Sea salt and pepper to taste

Preparation

1. Make four "ham-and-Swiss" roll-ups by tightly rolling two tablespoons shredded cheese inside two pieces of ham, folding in edges as needed. Cut a pocket through side of chicken into thickest part of each breast, then stuff each with one roll-up. Transfer chicken to a plate, cover with plastic wrap, and refrigerate until firm, at least 20 minutes or up to four hours.

2. Adjust oven rack to middle position; preheat oven to 425° F. Line a rimmed baking sheet with aluminum foil, top with wire rack, and grease rack with coconut oil. Spread almond flour in a shallow dish. In a second shallow dish, whisk eggs and Dijon Mustard together until foamy. In a third shallow dish, combine toasted breadcrumbs, almond flour, olive oil, ¼ teaspoon sea salt, and ¼ teaspoon pepper.

3. Working with one piece of chicken at a time, dredge in flour, dip into egg mixture, then coat with breadcrumb mixture, pressing gently to adhere; lay on prepared wire rack. Bake until chicken registers 160° F, about 30 minutes. Let chicken rest for 5 to 10 minutes; serve.

Cashew Chicken

SERVES 4

Ingredients

¼ cup Soy Sauce (see page 233)

2 tablespoons dry sherry

2 tablespoons tapioca or arrowroot starch

1 teaspoon palm sugar

4 teaspoons olive oil

12 ounces boneless, skinless chicken breasts, trimmed of all visible fat, halved lengthwise and sliced thin

¾ cup Chicken Broth or Stock (see page 236)

3 garlic cloves, minced

2 teaspoons grated fresh ginger

⅛ teaspoon red pepper flakes

1 red bell pepper, stemmed, seeded, and cut into 2-inch-long matchsticks

¼ cup water

8 ounces asparagus, tough ends trimmed

1 (8-ounce) can water chestnuts, drained and sliced thin

¼ cup roasted unsalted, cashews, coarsely chopped

Preparation

1. Whisk Soy Sauce, sherry, tapioca or arrowroot starch, and palm sugar together in a medium bowl. Measure two tablespoons of mixture into a separate bowl and stir in two teaspoons olive oil and chicken; let marinate for 10 to 30 minutes. Stir broth into remaining Soy Sauce mixture to make sauce; set aside. In separate bowl, combine garlic, ginger, pepper flakes, and remaining two teaspoons olive oil.

2. Submerge bell pepper in water, covered, in a twelve-inch nonstick skillet over high heat until water is boiling and pepper begins to soften, about 3 minutes. Uncover, add asparagus, and cook until water has evaporated and vegetables are crisp-tender, about 2 minutes; transfer to bowl.

3. Return now-empty skillet to medium-high heat. Add chicken with marinade, breaking up any clumps, and cook until lightly browned on all sides but not fully cooked, about 6 minutes. Clear center of skillet, add garlic mixture, and cook, mashing mixture into pan, until fragrant, 15 to 30 seconds.

4. Stir in water chestnuts and cashews. Whisk sauce to recombine and add to skillet. Simmer until chicken is cooked through and sauce is thickened, 30 seconds to 2 minutes. Add cooked vegetables and toss to coat. Serve.

{ Land and Ocean }

Oven-Fried Fish with Tartar Sauce

SERVES 4

Ingredients

Coconut oil for greasing baking rack

4 slices White Sandwich Bread, torn into pieces (see page 19)

1 tablespoon coconut oil

½ cup tapioca flour

¾ cup Tartar Sauce (see page 217)

2 large eggs

1 tablespoon Dijon Mustard (see page 225)

⅛ teaspoon cayenne pepper

2 tablespoons minced fresh parsley

Sea salt and pepper

1½ pounds skinless, wild-caught, thick whitefish fillets (cod, bass, tilapia, halibut, etc.), cut into 8 equal portions

---

Preparation

1. Adjust oven rack to middle position and preheat oven to 450° F. Line a rimmed baking sheet with aluminum foil, top with wire rack, and grease rack with oil. Pulse bread in food processor to create coarse crumbs, about 10 pulses. Toast breadcrumbs in oil in a twelve-inch nonstick skillet over medium heat, stirring often, until well browned, about 10 minutes; let cool.

2. Spread ¼ cup flour in a shallow dish. In a second shallow dish, whisk remaining ¼ cup flour, ¼ cup Tartar Sauce, eggs, Dijon Mustard, and cayenne together. In a third shallow dish, combine toasted breadcrumbs, parsley, ¼ teaspoon sea salt, and ⅛ teaspoon pepper.

3. Pat whitefish dry with paper towels and season with sea salt and pepper. Working with one piece of fish at a time and coating top and sides only, dredge in flour, dip in Tartar Sauce mixture, and then coat with bread crumbs, pressing gently to adhere; lay on prepared wire rack with uncoated side of fish facing down.

4. Bake until crumbs are golden and fish registers 140° F, 10 to 12 minutes. Serve with remaining ½ cup Tartar Sauce.

Oven-Fried Shrimp

SERVES 4

Ingredients

Coconut oil for greasing rack

½ cup tapioca or arrowroot flour

4 large eggs

1 teaspoon Dijon Mustard (see page 225)

1 cup White Sandwich Breadcrumbs, toasted (see page 19)

1 cup almond flour

2 tablespoons coconut oil

½ teaspoon sea salt

¼ teaspoon pepper

¼ teaspoon paprika

32 extra-large, wild-caught shrimp, peeled and deveined

Preparation

1. Adjust oven rack to middle position and preheat oven to 425° F. Line a rimmed baking sheet with aluminum foil, top with wire rack, and grease rack with oil. Spread flour in a shallow dish. In a second shallow dish, whisk eggs and Dijon Mustard together. In a third shallow dish, combine toasted breadcrumbs, almond flour, oil, sea salt, pepper, and paprika.

2. Pat shrimp dry with paper towels. Working in batches, dredge in tapioca flour, dip in egg mixture, and then coat with bread crumb mixture, pressing gently to adhere; lay on prepared wire rack. Bake until shrimp are cooked through, about 10 minutes. Serve.

Chef's Note: Shrimp come in a variety of sizes and are typically identified by count per pound. Use this chart determine which shrimp to purchase for the recipe.

Shrimp per pound:

- 10 shrimp or less = Colossal
- 11 to 15 = Jumbo
- 16 to 20 = Extra-large
- 21 to 30 = Large
- 31 to 35 = Medium
- 36 to 45 = Small
- about 100 = Miniature

Steak au Poivre with Brandied Cream Sauce

SERVES 4

Ingredients

4 (6-ounce) center-cut filets mignons, 1½ inches thick, trimmed of all visible fat

Sea salt and pepper

1 tablespoon black peppercorns, crushed

1 tablespoon coconut oil

1 shallot, minced

1 teaspoon minced fresh thyme

5 tablespoons brandy

1½ cups Chicken Broth or Stock (see page 236)

¼ cup coconut milk

2 teaspoons tapioca or arrowroot starch

Preparation

1. Adjust oven rack to middle position, place a rimmed baking sheet on oven rack, and preheat oven to 450° F. Pat steaks dry with paper towels and season with sea salt. Rub crushed peppercorns over one side of each steak, pressing gently to adhere.

2. Heat oil in a twelve-inch nonstick skillet over medium-high heat until just smoking. Lay steaks in skillet, peppered side up. Press firmly on steaks with bottom of cake pan and cook until well browned on bottom, about 3 minutes. Flip steaks; reduce heat to medium, and cook, pressing firmly with cake pan, until browned on second side, about 3 minutes. Transfer steaks to hot sheet, peppered side up, and roast until steaks register 120 to 125° F (for medium-rare), 4 to 6 minutes. Transfer steaks to carving board, tent loosely with aluminum foil, and let rest for 5 to 10 minutes.

3. Add shallot, thyme, and ¼ teaspoon sea salt to fat left in skillet and cook over medium heat until softened, about 2 minutes. Remove from heat and stir in ¼ cup brandy, scraping up any browned bits. Stir in broth and simmer over medium heat until sauce has reduced to ¾ cup, 5 to 7 minutes. Whisk coconut milk and tapioca or arrowroot starch together in bowl, then whisk into sauce and continue to simmer until slightly thickened, about 1 minute. Remove from heat, stir in remaining one tablespoon brandy, and season with sea salt and pepper to taste. Spoon sauce over filets and serve.

Steak Tips with Mushroom-Onion Gravy

SERVES 6

Ingredients

1½ pounds sirloin steak tips, trimmed of all visible fat and cut into 1½-inch chunks

1 tablespoon Soy Sauce (see page 233)

1 teaspoon palm sugar

Sea salt and pepper

4 teaspoons coconut oil

1 pound white mushrooms, trimmed and sliced thin

1 onion, halved and sliced thin or diced

¼ ounce dried porcini mushrooms, rinsed and minced

1 garlic clove, minced

½ teaspoon minced fresh thyme or ⅛ teaspoon dried thyme

4 teaspoons tapioca or arrowroot flour

1¾ cups Beef Broth or Stock (see page 236)

1 tablespoon minced fresh parsley

Preparation

1. Combine steak tips, Soy Sauce, palm sugar, and ⅛ teaspoon pepper in bowl; let marinate for 30 minutes to one hour. Heat two teaspoons oil in a twelve-inch skillet over medium-high heat until just smoking. Add marinated beef and cook until well browned on all sides, 4 to 6 minutes; transfer to plate.

2. Add remaining two teaspoons oil, white mushrooms, onion, porcini mushrooms, and ⅛ teaspoon sea salt to fat left in skillet. Cover and cook over medium-low heat until vegetables are softened, 8 to 10 minutes. Uncover, increase heat to medium-high, and continue to cook until vegetables are well browned, 8 to 12 minutes.

3. Stir in garlic and thyme and cook until fragrant, about 30 seconds. Stir in flour and cook for 1 minute. Stir in broth, scraping up any browned bits, and bring to a simmer. Add browned beef and any accumulated juices, reduce heat to medium-low, and simmer gently until meat registers 130 to 135° F (for medium), 3 to 5 minutes. Season with sea salt and pepper to taste, sprinkle with parsley, and serve.

Stir-Fried Beef and Broccoli with Classic Brown Stir-Fry Sauce

SERVES 4

Ingredients

Sauce
½ cup Chicken Broth or Stock (see page 236)

¼ cup Hoisin Sauce (see page 234)

3 tablespoons dry sherry

1 tablespoon Soy Sauce (see page 233)

1 tablespoon tapioca or arrowroot starch

Stir-Fry
12 ounces flank steak, trimmed of all visible fat and sliced thinly into 2-inch-long pieces

2 teaspoons Soy Sauce (see page 233)

3 scallions, minced

6 garlic cloves, minced

1 tablespoon grated fresh ginger

1 tablespoon coconut oil

1 pound broccoli, florets cut into 1-inch pieces, stalks peeled and sliced thin

⅓ cup water

2 red bell peppers, stemmed, seeded, and cut into 2-inch-long matchsticks

Preparation

1. **For the Sauce:** Whisk all ingredients together in bowl.

2. **For the Stir-Fry:** Combine beef and Soy Sauce in a bowl; marinate for 10 to 30 minutes. In a separate bowl, combine scallions, garlic, ginger, and one teaspoon coconut oil.

3. Cook broccoli florets, broccoli stalks, and water together in a covered twelve-inch nonstick skillet over high heat until the water is boiling and broccoli is green and beginning to soften, about 2 minutes. Uncover, add bell peppers, and cook until water has evaporated and vegetables are crisp-tender, about 3 minutes; transfer to colander.

4. Add remaining two teaspoons coconut oil to now-empty skillet and place over high heat until just smoking. Add beef with marinade, breaking up any clumps, and cook until lightly browned on all sides but not fully cooked, about 2 minutes.

Clear center of skillet, add garlic mixture, and cook, mashing mixture into pan, until fragrant, 15 to 30 seconds.

5. Stir in cooked vegetables. Whisk sauce to recombine and add to skillet. Simmer until beef is cooked through and sauce is thickened, about 1 minute. Serve.

Beef Stroganoff

SERVES 6

Ingredients

Coconut oil for greasing baking sheet

1½ pounds portobello mushroom caps, gills removed, caps halved and sliced thin

½ cup cold water

Sea salt and pepper

1 teaspoon baking soda

1¼ pounds sirloin steak, trimmed of all visible fat and sliced thinly into 2-inch-long pieces

1 tablespoon coconut oil

1 onion, chopped fine

4 teaspoons tapioca or arrowroot flour

2 teaspoons tomato paste

1½ cups Beef Broth or Stock (see page 236)

3 tablespoons white wine

2 teaspoons Dijon Mustard

½ cup coconut milk

1 large egg white

1 tablespoon minced fresh parsley

Preparation

1. Adjust oven rack to middle position and preheat oven to 425° F. Grease rimmed baking sheet with oil. Spread sliced mushrooms over prepared baking sheet, sprinkle with ¼ teaspoon sea salt and ¼ teaspoon pepper. Roast, stirring occasionally, until golden, about 15 minutes.

2. Meanwhile, combine ½ cup cold water and baking soda in a large bowl, add beef, and let sit for 15 minutes to tenderize.

3. Drain and rinse tenderized beef; pat dry with paper towels. Heat one teaspoon oil in a twelve-inch nonstick skillet over high heat until just smoking. Add half of beef and cook without stirring until browned around edges, 1 to 2 minutes. Stir and continue to cook beef until no longer pink, about 30 seconds; transfer to clean bowl. Repeat with one teaspoon oil and remaining beef.

4. Add remaining one teaspoon oil, onion, and ¼ teaspoon sea salt to fat left in skillet; cook over medium heat until browned, 6 to 8 minutes. Stir in roasted mushrooms, flour, and tomato paste and cook until tomato paste begins to darken, about 2 minutes. Stir in broth, wine, and Dijon Mustard, scraping up

any browned bits, and bring to a boil. Reduce heat to medium-low and simmer gently until sauce is slightly thickened, about 5 minutes.

5. Stir browned beef and any accumulated juices into skillet; simmer gently until heated through, about 1 minute. Remove from heat, whisk milk and egg white together, then stir into skillet. Stir in parsley; season with sea salt and pepper to taste. Serve warm.

Meatloaf

SERVES 6

Ingredients

1 teaspoon coconut oil

1 onion, chopped fine

Sea salt and pepper to taste

10 ounces cremini or white mushrooms, trimmed and sliced thin

3 garlic cloves, minced

1 teaspoon minced fresh thyme

¼ cup tomato juice

1 slice White Sandwich Bread, torn into pieces (see page 19)

1½ pounds ground beef

1 large egg

2 tablespoons minced fresh parsley

1 tablespoon Soy Sauce (see page 233)

1 tablespoon Dijon Mustard (see page 225)

⅓ cup Ketchup (see page 221)

3 tablespoons cider vinegar

2 tablespoons packed palm sugar

1 teaspoon Louisiana-Style Fermented Hot Pepper Sauce (see page 226)

Preparation

1. Adjust oven rack to middle position and preheat oven to 375°F. Set wire rack inside a rimmed baking sheet and arrange an 8x6-inch piece of aluminum foil in center of rack. Using a skewer, poke holes in foil every half-inch.

2. Heat oil in a twelve-inch nonstick skillet over medium heat until shimmering. Add onion and ¼ teaspoon sea salt and cook until softened, about 5 minutes. Stir in mushrooms and cook until they have released their liquid and are lightly browned, about 10 minutes. Stir in garlic and thyme and cook until fragrant, about 30 seconds. Stir in tomato juice and cook until thickened, about 1 minute. Let mixture cool for 5 minutes; transfer to a food processor and add bread, then process until smooth, about 25 seconds. Add ground beef and pulse to combine, about 20 pulses.

3. Whisk egg, parsley, Soy Sauce, Dijon Mustard, ¼ teaspoon sea salt, and ½ teaspoon pepper in large bowl. Add processed beef mixture and mix with hands until evenly combined. Using hands, shape mixture into 8x6-inch loaf on top of prepared foil. Bake until meatloaf registers 160° F, about 1 hour.

4. Simmer Ketchup, vinegar, palm sugar, and Louisiana-Style Fermented Hot Pepper Sauce together in small saucepan until thickened, about 5 minutes. Remove meatloaf from oven, adjust oven rack to a position eight inches from broiler element, and heat broiler. Spread glaze over baked meatloaf and broil until glaze begins to bubble, about 3 minutes. Let rest for 10 minutes. Serve.

Chicken-Fried Steak

SERVES 4

Ingredients

Coconut oil for greasing wire rack

½ cup tapioca or arrowroot flour

4 large eggs

1 cup White Sandwich Breadcrumbs, toasted

1 cup almond flour

1 teaspoon onion powder

1 tablespoon coconut oil

Sea salt and pepper to taste

⅛ teaspoon cayenne pepper

2 (1-pound) boneless strip steaks, trimmed of all visible fat, each steak halved

4 ounces turkey breakfast sausage, chopped fine, or ground chicken sausage

1½ cups coconut milk

2 teaspoons tapioca or arrowroot starch

Preparation

1. Adjust oven rack to middle position and preheat oven to 425° F. Line a rimmed baking sheet with aluminum foil, top with wire rack, and grease rack with coconut oil. Spread flour in a shallow dish. In a second shallow dish, whisk eggs until foamy. In a third shallow dish, combine toasted breadcrumbs, almond flour, onion powder, oil, ¼ teaspoon sea salt, ¼ teaspoon pepper, and cayenne.

2. Pound steaks to a half-inch thickness with a meat mallet, then pat dry with paper towels and season with sea salt and pepper. Working with one steak at a time, dredge in flour, dip in eggs, then coat with breadcrumb mixture, pressing gently to adhere; lay on prepared wire rack. Roast steaks until meat registers 150 to 155° F, about 10 minutes.

3. Meanwhile, cook sausage in a medium saucepan over medium heat until no longer pink, about 5 minutes. Stir in one cup of milk and simmer gently for 5 minutes. Combine remaining ½ cup milk and tapioca or arrowroot starch, then whisk into pot. Continue to simmer sauce, whisking constantly, until thickened. Season with sea salt and pepper to taste. Spoon sauce over steak and serve.

Stuffed Bell Peppers

SERVES 4

Ingredients

Coconut oil for greasing baking pan

4 (6-ounce) red, yellow, or orange bell
    peppers, ½ inch trimmed off tops,
    stemmed, and seeded

Sea salt and pepper

1 teaspoon olive oil

1 onion, chopped fine

12 ounces lean ground turkey or lean

ground beef

3 garlic cloves, minced

1 (14.5-ounce) can diced tomatoes,
    drained, with ¼ cup juice reserved

2 ounces Coconut Milk Cheddar Cheese,
    grated (see page 239)

¼ cup minced fresh parsley

¼ cup Ketchup (see page 221)

Preparation

1. Adjust oven rack to middle position and preheat oven to 350° F. Grease baking pan with coconut oil. Bring four quarts water to boil in a large pot. Add bell peppers and one tablespoon sea salt and cook until peppers just begin to soften, about 3 minutes. Remove peppers from water, drain well, then place cut side up on a clean towel to allow the steam to escape.

2. Combine oil, onion, and ½ teaspoon sea salt in a twelve-inch nonstick skillet, cover, and cook over medium-low heat until onion is softened, 8 to 10 minutes. Stir in ground turkey or beef and cook, breaking up meat with a wooden spoon, until no longer pink, about 4 minutes. Stir in garlic and cook until fragrant, about 30 seconds. Stir in tomatoes and cook until warmed through, about 2 minutes. Transfer mixture to a bowl with rice. Stir in cheese and parsley and season with sea salt and pepper to taste.

3. Drain excess water from peppers, arrange in an eight-inch square baking dish, and pack each with filling. Combine Ketchup and reserved tomato juice, then spoon over top. Bake until filling is hot, 25 to 30 minutes. Serve.

Stuffed Pork Chops

SERVES 4

Ingredients

4 (6-ounce) boneless pork chops or
pork tenderloin, about 1 inch thick,
trimmed of all visible fat

4 teaspoons baking soda

1 tablespoon palm sugar

Sea salt and pepper

1 teaspoon coconut oil

½ small fennel bulb, stalks discarded,
cored, and chopped fine

1 shallot, minced

2 garlic cloves, minced

2 tablespoons dry white wine

6 ounces (6 cups) baby spinach

1½ ounces Coconut Milk Cheddar Cheese,
crumbled (see page 239)

¼ teaspoon grated lemon zest

1 teaspoon fennel seeds, toasted and
crushed

1 teaspoon ground coriander

½ teaspoon ground cumin

Vegetable oil spray

Preparation

1. Working with one chop or tenderloin at a time, use a paring knife to cut one-inch openings in the side of each chop. Through opening, continue to cut a large pocket inside center of chop for filling; use fingers to help enlarge pocket if necessary. Repeat with remaining chops. Combine two cups water, baking soda, palm sugar, and one tablespoon sea salt in a large container. Add chops and refrigerate for 30 minutes.

2. Adjust oven rack to upper-middle position, place a rimmed baking sheet on rack, and preheat oven to 475° F. Heat oil in a twelve-inch nonstick skillet over medium heat until shimmering. Add fennel, shallot, and ¼ teaspoon sea salt and cook until lightly browned, about 5 minutes. Stir in garlic and cook until fragrant, about 30 seconds. Stir in wine and cook until it evaporates, about 1 minute. Stir in spinach and cook until wilted, about 2 minutes. Transfer to bowl, allow to cool for 5 minutes, and then stir in cheese and lemon zest. Season with sea salt and pepper to taste.

3. Remove chops or tenderloin from brine, rinse, and pat dry with paper towels. Using a spoon and your fingers, gently stuff chops with spinach filling. Combine crushed fennel seeds, coriander, cumin, and ½ teaspoon pepper in bowl, and then rub evenly over chops or tenderloin. Spray both sides of chops or tenderloin with oil spray. Lay chops on preheated sheet and bake until pork registers 145° F, 10 to 14 minutes, flipping chops halfway through cooking. Transfer chops or tenderloin to carving board, tent loosely with aluminum foil, and let rest for 5 to 10 minutes. Serve.

Smothered Pork Chops

Serves 4

Ingredients

Coconut oil for greasing rimmed
  baking sheet
4 (8-ounce) bone-in pork rib chops, ½- to
  ¾-inch thick, trimmed of all visible fat
Sea salt and pepper
1 slice bacon, cut into ¼-inch pieces
2 onions, halved and sliced thin

2 tablespoons water
2 garlic cloves, minced
1 teaspoon minced fresh thyme
2 tablespoons tapioca or arrowroot flour
1¾ cups Beef Broth or Stock or Stock (see
  page 236)
2 bay leaves

Preparation

1. Pat pork dry with paper towels and season with pepper. Preheat oven to 425° F. Grease baking sheet with coconut oil.

2. Cook bacon in a twelve-inch nonstick skillet over medium heat until crisp, 5 to 7 minutes; transfer to paper towel-lined plate. Heat bacon fat left in skillet over high heat until just smoking. Add pork and brown well on both sides, about 2 minutes; transfer to a baking sheet and place in oven for 5 to 7 minutes or until pork registers 145° F on a meat thermometer in center of chop.

3. Add onions and ¼ teaspoon sea salt to fat left in skillet and cook over medium heat, scraping up any browned bits, until softened, 5 to 7 minutes. Stir in garlic and thyme and cook until fragrant, about 30 seconds. Whisk in broth, increase heat to medium-high, and bring to a boil.

4. Add bay leaves, cooked bacon, and any accumulated juices and cover chops with onions and sauce. Cover, reduce heat to low, and simmer gently until pork is very tender, 30 to 35 minutes.

5. Whisk tapioca into water and set aside.

6. Transfer chops to a serving platter and tent loosely with aluminum foil. Whisk tapioca flour mixture into sauce and continue to simmer until thickened. Remove bay leaves and season with sea salt and pepper to taste. Spoon sauce over pork chops and serve.

Spicy Mexican Shredded Pork Tostadas

SERVES 6

Ingredients

1 pound boneless pork butt roast, trimmed of all visible fat and cut into 1-inch chunks

2 onions, 1 quartered and 1 chopped fine

5 garlic cloves, peeled, 3 smashed and 2 minced

4 sprigs fresh thyme

2 bay leaves

12 (6-inch) Tortillas (see page 32)

Enough coconut oil for cooking turnips, mushrooms, and pork, and greasing baking sheets

½ teaspoon dried oregano

1 (15-ounce) can tomato sauce

1½ cups water

8 ounces cremini mushrooms

7 ounces turnips

1 tablespoon minced canned chipotle chilies in adobo sauce (paleo-friendly)

Sea salt and pepper

Preparation

1. Bring four cups water, pork, quartered onion, smashed garlic, thyme, and bay leaves to simmer in a large saucepan over medium-high heat, skimming off any foam that rises to the surface. Reduce heat to medium-low, partially cover, and cook until meat is tender, one hour and 15 to 30 minutes.

2. Heat oil in a nonstick skillet over medium heat until shimmering. Add mushrooms and cook until they release their liquid. Continue to cook until well cooked, tender, and slightly browned. Set aside.

3. Place 1½ cups of water and turnips in a pot over medium-high heat and cover. Bring to a boil, then reduce to medium low heat and simmer until crisp and tender. Drain and set aside.

4. Meanwhile, adjust oven racks to upper-middle and lower-middle positions and preheat oven to 450° F. Spread Tortillas over two rimmed baking sheets, grease both sides with oil, and bake until brown and crisp, 8 to 10 minutes, switching and rotating sheets halfway through baking.

5. Drain pork, reserving one cup of cooking liquid. Remove onion, garlic, thyme, and bay leaves. Return pork to saucepan and, using a potato masher, mash until pork is shredded into rough ½-inch pieces.

6. Heat oil in a twelve-inch nonstick skillet over medium-high heat until just smoking. Add shredded pork and chopped onion and cook until pork is well-browned and crisp, 5 to 7 minutes. Stir in minced garlic and oregano and cook until fragrant, about 30 seconds. Stir in reserved pork cooking liquid, tomato sauce, mushrooms, turnips, and chipotle. Bring to a simmer and cook until almost all the liquid has evaporated, 5 to 7 minutes; season with sea salt and pepper to taste. Spoon pork mixture onto tostadas and serve.

Baked Stuffed Shrimp

SERVES 4

Ingredients

24 jumbo shrimp, wild-caught, peeled and deveined

2 tablespoons coconut oil

5 scallions, chopped fine

1 large celery rib, chopped fine

2 garlic cloves, minced

¾ teaspoon ground coriander

2 tablespoons dry white wine

5 tablespoons Mayonnaise (see page 214)

¼ cup White Sandwich Breadcrumbs, toasted (see page 19)

3 tablespoons minced fresh parsley

1 teaspoon grated lemon zest

4 teaspoons lemon juice

Sea salt and pepper to taste

¼ teaspoon palm sugar

Preparation

1. Remove and discard tails from eight shrimp, then pulse in a food processor until coarsely chopped, about 4 pulses; transfer to a large bowl.

2. Melt coconut oil in a twelve-inch nonstick skillet over medium heat. Add scallions and celery and cook until softened, about 5 minutes. Stir in garlic and ¼ teaspoon coriander and cook until fragrant, about 30 seconds. Stir in wine and cook until nearly evaporated, about 1 minute; transfer to bowl with processed shrimp. Stir in Mayonnaise, breadcrumbs, parsley, lemon zest and juice, ⅛ teaspoon sea salt, and ⅛ teaspoon pepper until well combined.

3. Adjust oven rack to middle position and preheat oven to 275° F. Line a rimmed baking sheet with aluminum foil and grease with oil. Combine remaining ½ teaspoon coriander, palm sugar, pinch sea salt, and ¼ teaspoon pepper in a large bowl. Pat remaining sixteen shrimp dry with paper towels and toss with spice mixture. Using a paring knife, butterfly shrimp open through vein side. Cut a one-inch slit through the center of each shrimp so that they lay flat.

4. Lay shrimp butterflied side down on prepared sheet. Divide filling among shrimp, press gently on filling to compact, then flip tail back to curl around filling. Bake until shrimp are cooked through and filling is hot, 20 to 25 minutes. Serve.

Chef's Note: Shrimp come in a variety of sizes and are typically identified by count per pound. Use this chart determine which shrimp to purchase for the recipe. Shrimp per pound:

- 10 shrimp or less = Colossal
- 11 to 15 = Jumbo
- 16 to 20 = Extra-large
- 21 to 30 = Large
- 31 to 35 = Medium
- 36 to 45 = Small
- about 100 = Miniature

Stir-Fried Shrimp and Asparagus with Coconut Curry Sauce

SERVES 4

Ingredients

Sauce

⅔ cup coconut milk

6 tablespoons Chicken Broth or Stock (see page 236)

1 tablespoon tapioca or arrowroot starch

2 teaspoons curry powder

1 teaspoon palm sugar

¼ teaspoon sea salt

⅛ teaspoon red pepper flakes

2 teaspoons Soy Sauce (see page 233)

3 scallions, minced

3 garlic cloves, minced

1 tablespoon grated fresh ginger

4 teaspoons coconut oil

2 red bell peppers, stemmed, seeded, and cut into 2-inch-long matchsticks

⅓ cup water

12 ounces asparagus, tough ends removed and cut into 2-inch-long pieces

Stir-Fry

1 pound extra-large shrimp, wild-caught, peeled and deveined

Preparation

1. **For the Sauce:** Whisk all ingredients together in a bowl.
2. **For the Stir-Fry:** Toss shrimp and Soy Sauce together in a bowl; marinate for 10 to 30 minutes. In a separate bowl, combine scallions, garlic, ginger, and one teaspoon oil.
3. Cook bell peppers and water together in a covered twelve-inch nonstick skillet over high heat until water is boiling and peppers begin to soften, about 3 minutes. Uncover, add asparagus, and cook until water has evaporated and vegetables are crisp-tender, about 2 minutes; transfer to colander.
4. Add remaining one tablespoon oil to now-empty skillet and place over high heat until just shimmering. Add shrimp with marinade and cook until lightly browned on all sides but not fully cooked, about 2 minutes. Clear center of

skillet, add garlic mixture, and cook, mashing mixture into pan, until fragrant, 15 to 30 seconds.

5. Stir in cooked vegetables. Whisk sauce to recombine and add to skillet. Simmer until shrimp are cooked through and sauce is thickened, about 1 minute. Serve.

Chef's Note: Shrimp come in a variety of sizes and are typically identified by count per pound. Use this chart determine which shrimp to purchase for the recipe.

Shrimp per pound:

- 10 shrimp or less = Colossal
- 11 to 15 = Jumbo
- 16 to 20 = Extra-large
- 21 to 30 = Large
- 31 to 35 = Medium
- 36 to 45 = Small
- about 100 = Miniature

Crab-Stuffed Flounder

SERVES 4

Ingredients

1 tablespoon coconut oil

3 scallions, white parts chopped fine, green parts sliced thin on bias

1 celery rib, minced

½ red bell pepper, chopped fine

1 garlic clove, minced

¾ teaspoon Cajun seasoning

3 ounces Coconut Milk Cheddar Cheese, cut into small pieces (see page 239)

12 ounces lump crabmeat, picked over for shells

2 cups fresh spinach, stemmed

Sea salt and pepper to taste

8 (3-ounce) skinless flounder fillets, ¼- to ½-inch thick

¼ cup White Sandwich Breadcrumbs, toasted (see page 19)

Preparation

1. Adjust oven rack to middle position and preheat oven to 475° F. Heat two teaspoons oil in ten-inch nonstick skillet over medium heat until shimmering. Add scallion whites, celery, and bell pepper and cook until softened, about 5 minutes. Stir in garlic and Cajun seasoning and cook until fragrant, about 30 seconds. Remove from heat and stir in cheese until melted; transfer to a large bowl. Gently stir in crabmeat and spinach, being careful not to break up lumps of crab. Season with sea salt and pepper to taste.

2. Grease a 13x9-inch baking dish with coconut oil. Pat flounder dry with paper towels and season with sea salt and pepper. Place flounder, smooth side down, on cutting board. Mound filling in center of fillets, fold tail end over filling, and then fold over thicker end. Lay flounder seam-side down in baking dish.

3. Toss breadcrumbs with remaining one teaspoon oil, then sprinkle over flounder. Bake until filling is hot and flounder flakes apart when gently prodded with a paring knife, about 20 minutes. Sprinkle with scallion greens and serve.

Crab Cakes

SERVES 4

Ingredients

Coconut oil for greasing foil

⅔ cups White Sandwich Breadcrumbs (see page 19)

1 pound lump crabmeat, picked over for shells

3 scallions, minced

3 tablespoons Mayonnaise (see page 214)

1 tablespoon coconut oil

1 large egg white

1½ teaspoons Dijon Mustard (see page 225)

1 teaspoon Louisiana-Style Fermented Hot Pepper Sauce (see page 226)

1 teaspoon Old Bay seasoning

Preparation

1. Using a rubber spatula, gently combine crabmeat, ¼ cup processed breadcrumbs, scallions, Mayonnaise, coconut oil, egg white, Dijon Mustard, Louisiana-Style Fermented Hot Pepper Sauce, and Old Bay seasoning in a bowl.
2. Divide mixture into four equal portions and shape into tight, mounded cakes. Transfer to a large plate. Cover and refrigerate for one to eight hours.
3. Adjust oven rack to a position six inches from broiler element and heat broiler. Line a rimmed baking sheet with aluminum foil and grease with oil. Transfer crab cakes to prepared sheet, crumb side down. Broil crab cakes until golden, 12 to 15 minutes. Serve.

{ Vegetarian Main Course }

Eggplant Parmesan with Spaghetti Squash	150	Pasta with Sautéed Mushrooms	155
Spaghetti Squash with		Pasta Primavera	156
Creamy Basil Pesto	152	Spaghetti Squash Carbonara	158

Eggplant Parmesan with Spaghetti Squash

Serves 6

Ingredients

Coconut oil

2 pounds eggplant, sliced into ⅓-inch-
thick rounds

Sea salt and pepper

½ cup tapioca or arrowroot flour

3 large egg whites

1½ cups White Sandwich Breadcrumbs,
toasted (see page 19)

1 tablespoon extra-virgin olive oil

1½ teaspoons garlic powder

4 cups tomato sauce

1 tablespoon dried oregano

8 ounces Coconut Milk Cheddar Cheese,
shredded (see page 239)

2 tablespoons chopped fresh basil

12 ounces Spaghetti Squash, prepared
(see page 59)

Preparation

1. Adjust oven racks to upper-middle and lower-middle positions and preheat oven
    to 475° F. Line two rimmed baking sheets with aluminum foil, top with wire
    racks, and grease racks with oil. Working with half of eggplant at a time, toss in a
    bowl with ½ teaspoon sea salt and transfer to a large colander (use one teaspoon
    sea salt total); allow to drain for 30 minutes. Spread eggplant over several layers
    of paper towels and pat dry thoroughly.

2. Spread tapioca flour in a shallow dish. In a second shallow dish, whisk egg
    whites until foamy. In a third shallow dish, combine toasted breadcrumbs, garlic
    powder, and ½ teaspoon sea salt.

3. Season eggplant with ½ teaspoon pepper. Working with one eggplant slice at
    a time and coating the tops only, dredge in flour, dip in eggs, then coat with
    breadcrumb mixture, pressing gently to adhere; lay on prepared wire racks
    with breaded side of eggplant facing up. Bake until eggplant is tender, about
    30 minutes.

4. Mix oregano with tomato sauce and spread ½ cup tomato sauce over bottom
    of a 13x9-inch baking dish. Lay half of eggplant slices in dish, breaded side up,
    overlapping as needed to fit. Spoon ½ cup sauce over top and sprinkle with one cup

cheese. Layer remaining eggplant over top, breaded side up, and dot with one cup sauce, leaving majority of eggplant exposed. Sprinkle with remaining one cup cheese. Bake until sauce is bubbling and cheese is browned, about 10 minutes. Let cool for 5 minutes, and then sprinkle with basil.

5. Stir prepared spaghetti squash with remaining two cups tomato sauce, season with sea salt and pepper to taste. Serve with eggplant.

Spaghetti Squash with Creamy Basil Pesto

SERVES 6

Ingredients

---

4 garlic cloves, unpeeled

3 cups fresh basil leaves

⅛ cup coconut milk

1 shallot, minced

2 tablespoons extra-virgin olive oil

1 pound Spaghetti Squash, prepared (see page 59)

Preparation

1. Toast garlic in a small skillet over medium heat, shaking pan occasionally, until color of cloves deepens slightly, about 7 minutes; transfer to a plate and allow to cool slightly, then peel and mince.

2. Place basil in a heavy-duty, zipper storage bag and pound with a meat mallet or rolling pin until leaves are lightly bruised. Process toasted garlic, bruised basil, coconut milk, shallot, oil, and ½ teaspoon sea salt in a food processor until smooth, about 30 seconds, scraping down bowl as needed.

3. Stir prepared spaghetti squash with pesto and season with sea salt and pepper to taste. Serve.

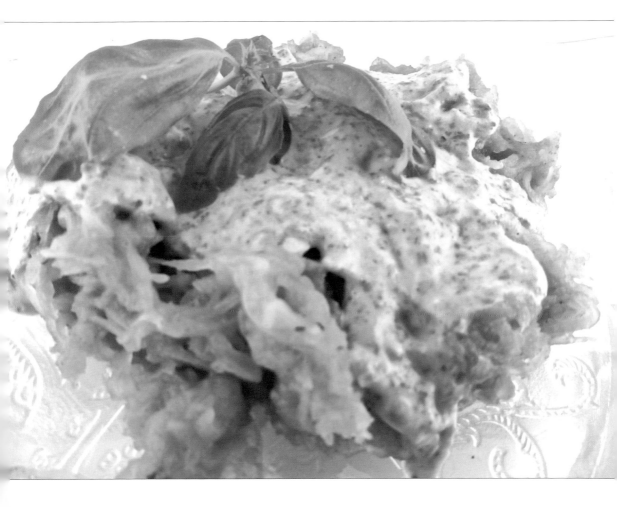

Pasta with Sautéed Mushrooms

SERVES 6

Ingredients

1 teaspoon extra-virgin olive oil

12 ounces shiitake mushrooms, stemmed and sliced ¼ inch thick

12 ounces cremini mushrooms, trimmed and sliced ¼ inch thick

½ onion, chopped fine

Sea salt and pepper

3 garlic cloves, minced

4 teaspoons minced fresh thyme

2 ounces coconut milk

1¼ cups Vegetable Broth or Stock (see page 236)

½ ounce dried porcini mushrooms, rinsed and minced

1 pound Spaghetti Squash, prepared (see page 59)

2 tablespoons minced fresh parsley

Preparation

1. Heat oil in a twelve-inch skillet over medium heat until shimmering. Add shiitakes, cremini, onion, and ¼ teaspoon sea salt, cover, and cook until mushrooms have released their liquid, about 8 minutes. Uncover and continue to cook until mushrooms are dry and browned, about 8 minutes. Stir in garlic and thyme and cook until fragrant, about 30 seconds; transfer to a bowl and cover.

2. Add broth and porcini to now-empty skillet, scraping up any browned bits, and simmer until porcini are softened, about 2 minutes. Remove from heat, whisk in coconut milk, and season with sea salt and pepper to taste; cover and set aside.

3. Stir together spaghetti squash, cooked vegetables, porcini mixture, and parsley, then season with sea salt and pepper to taste. Serve.

Pasta Primavera

Ingredients

1½ pounds leeks, white and light green parts halved lengthwise, sliced ½-inch thick, and washed thoroughly; 3 cups dark green parts, chopped coarse and washed thoroughly

1 pound asparagus, trimmed, tough ends reserved and chopped coarse; spears sliced ½-inch thick on bias

2 cups turnips, diced

4 garlic cloves, minced

4 cups vegetable broth (see page 237)

1 cup water, plus extra as needed

2 tablespoons extra-virgin olive oil

⅛ teaspoon red pepper flakes

1 pound Spaghetti Squash, prepared (see page 59)

1 cup dry white wine

2 tablespoons minced fresh mint (optional)

2 tablespoons minced fresh chives

½ teaspoon grated lemon zest

1 tablespoon lemon juice, fresh squeezed

Preparation

1. Place dark green leek trimmings, asparagus trimmings, one cup turnips, half of garlic, vegetable broth, and water in large saucepan. Bring to a simmer and cook gently for 10 minutes. Strain broth through a fine-mesh strainer into an eight-cup liquid measuring cup, pressing on solids to extract as much liquid as possible; discard solids. (You should have five cups of broth; add water as needed to measure five cups.) Return broth to saucepan, cover, and keep warm over low heat.

2. Combine sliced leeks, one teaspoon oil, and ⅛ teaspoon sea salt in a Dutch oven. Cover and cook over medium-low heat, stirring occasionally, until just beginning to brown, about 5 minutes. Stir in asparagus pieces and cook until crisp-tender, 4 to 6 minutes. Stir in remaining garlic and pepper flakes and cook until fragrant, about 30 seconds. Stir in remaining one cup turnips and cook for 1 minute; transfer vegetables to a plate.

3. Wipe now-empty pot clean, add two teaspoons oil, and place over medium heat until shimmering. Add spaghetti squash and cook, stirring frequently, until just

beginning to brown. Stir in wine and warm broth, increase heat to medium-high, and bring to a boil. Simmer, stirring often, until most of the liquid is absorbed and spaghetti squash is almost dry, about 15 minutes. Meanwhile, combine mint, chives, and lemon zest in bowl.

4. Remove from heat and add in cooked vegetables, spaghetti squash, remaining one tablespoon oil, half of herb mixture, and lemon juice, then season with sea salt and pepper to taste. Serve, passing remaining herb mixture separately.

Spaghetti Squash Alfredo

SERVES 4

Ingredients

Sea salt and pepper to taste

Pinch of nutmeg

1½ tablespoons olive oil or coconut oil, melted

1 tablespoon tapioca or arrowroot flour

1 cup coconut milk

1 garlic clove, peeled and lightly crushed

1 cup Coconut Milk Cheddar Cheese, grated (see page 239)

1 pound fresh Spaghetti Squash, prepared (see page 59)

Preparation

1. Bring four quarts water to boil in large pot. Using a ladle, fill four individual serving bowls with about ½ cup boiling water; set aside.

2. Whisk together oil, milk, garlic, ½ teaspoon sea salt, ½ teaspoon pepper, and nutmeg. Remove from heat, discard garlic, and stir in cheese; cover and set aside.

3. Return alfredo sauce to low heat and stir in cooked spaghetti squash. Cook gently, tossing pasta with tongs, until everything is heated through and sauce nicely coats pasta, about 1 minute. Season with sea salt and pepper to taste. Working quickly, empty water from serving bowls, fill with pasta, and serve immediately.

{ Pasta }

Spaghetti Squash Carbonara

Ingredients

Sea salt and pepper to taste

¼ cup coconut milk

2 tablespoons Mayonnaise (see page 214)

2 large eggs

2 slices bacon, chopped

3 garlic cloves, minced

⅓ cup dry white wine

¼ cup chicken stock

1 pound Spaghetti Squash, prepared (see page 59)

1 tablespoon minced fresh parsley

Preparation

1. Process coconut milk, 1½ tablespoons Mayonnaise, and eggs in a food processor until smooth, about 15 seconds; leave in processor.

2. Cook bacon in a twelve-inch nonstick skillet over medium heat until fat has rendered and bacon is browned, about 7 minutes; transfer to paper towel–lined plate. Add garlic and one teaspoon pepper to fat left in skillet and cook over medium heat until fragrant, about 30 seconds. Stir in wine and simmer until thickened slightly, about 1 minute; cover and set aside.

3. Stir remaining 1½ teaspoons Mayonnaise into spaghetti squash.

4. With processor running, slowly add wine mixture and ¼ cup chicken stock to Mayonnaise mixture and process until smooth and frothy, about 1 minute. Immediately stir mixture into spaghetti squash and season with sea salt and pepper to taste. Stir in crisp bacon, sprinkle with parsley, and serve.

Weeknight Sausage Ragu

Serves 6

Ingredients

Sea salt and pepper to taste

2 (28-ounce) cans diced tomatoes

1 tablespoon olive oil

2 onions, chopped

5 garlic cloves, minced

1 tablespoon tomato paste

¼ cup red wine

1 red bell pepper, stemmed, seeded, and chopped

12 ounces hot Italian turkey sausage, casings removed

1 pound Spaghetti Squash, prepared (see page 59)

¼ cup chopped fresh basil

Preparation

1. Working in batches, pulse tomatoes with their juices in a food processor until mostly smooth, about 10 pulses; transfer to a bowl. Heat oil in a large saucepan over medium-high heat until shimmering. Add onions and ¼ teaspoon sea salt and cook until golden brown, about 7 minutes.

2. Stir in garlic and tomato paste and cook until fragrant, about 1 minute. Stir in wine, scraping up any browned bits. Stir in bell pepper and sausage and cook, breaking up meat with a wooden spoon, until sausage is no longer pink, about 4 minutes. Stir in processed tomatoes and simmer sauce until thickened, about 45 minutes.

3. Place spaghetti squash in large bowl, stir in sauce and basil, and season with sea salt and pepper to taste. Serve.

Spaghetti and Meatballs

SERVES 6

Ingredients

Sea salt and pepper to taste

½ cup White Sandwich Breadcrumbs (see page 19)

¼ cup coconut milk

1 ounce Coconut Milk Cheddar Cheese, grated (see page 239)

¼ cup minced fresh parsley

6 garlic cloves, minced

1 pound 93% lean ground turkey

3 (14.5-ounce) cans diced tomatoes

2 teaspoons coconut oil

1 onion, chopped fine

¼ teaspoon red pepper flakes

1 pound Spaghetti Squash, prepared (see page 59)

3 tablespoons chopped fresh basil

Preparation

1. Mix breadcrumbs, milk, cheese, parsley, one-third of garlic, ½ teaspoon sea salt, and ½ teaspoon pepper together in bowl. Add turkey and mix with hands until evenly combined. Lightly shape mixture into twelve 1½-inch meatballs.

2. Pulse two cans tomatoes with their juices in a food processor until mostly smooth, about 10 pulses. Heat oil in a twelve-inch nonstick skillet over medium heat until shimmering. Brown meatballs well on all sides, about 10 minutes; transfer to paper towel-lined plate.

3. Add onion and ⅛ teaspoon sea salt to fat left in skillet, cover, and cook over medium-low heat until softened, 8 to 10 minutes. Stir in remaining garlic and pepper flakes and cook until fragrant, about 30 seconds. Stir in processed tomatoes and remaining can of diced tomatoes with their juices and simmer for 10 minutes. Return meatballs to skillet, cover, and simmer until meatballs are cooked through, about 10 minutes.

4. Place spaghetti squash in a bowl and stir in several large spoonfuls of tomato sauce, seasoning with sea salt and pepper to taste. Divide pasta among individual bowls, top with meatballs and remaining sauce, and sprinkle with basil. Serve.

Linguine with Bolognese Sauce

SERVES 6

Ingredients

Sea salt and pepper to taste

2 carrots, peeled and cut into 1-inch pieces

1 onion, chopped

2 ounces pancetta, cut into 1-inch pieces

½ ounce dried porcini mushrooms, rinsed

1 anchovy fillet, rinsed

1 (28-ounce) can whole tomatoes

1 tablespoon coconut oil

1 teaspoon sugar

1 garlic clove, minced

1 pound 93% lean ground turkey

1½ cups coconut milk

2 tablespoons tomato paste

½ cup dry white wine

1 pound Spaghetti Squash, prepared (see page 59)

Preparation

1. Pulse carrots and onion in a food processor until finely chopped, 10 to 15 pulses; transfer to a bowl. Process pancetta, mushrooms, and anchovy in now-empty food processor until finely chopped, 30 to 35 seconds; transfer to a separate bowl. Pulse tomatoes with their juices in now-empty food processor until mostly smooth, about 8 pulses; transfer to a third bowl.

2. Melt coconut oil in a Dutch oven over medium heat. Add processed pancetta mixture and cook until browned, about 2 minutes. Stir in processed carrot mixture and one teaspoon sea salt, cover, and cook over medium-low heat, stirring occasionally, until softened, 8 to 10 minutes.

3. Stir in palm sugar and garlic and cook until fragrant, about 30 seconds. Stir in turkey, breaking up meat with a wooden spoon, and cook for 1 minute. Stir in milk, scraping up any browned bits, and simmer, stirring occasionally, until nearly evaporated, 18 to 20 minutes.

4. Stir in tomato paste and cook for 1 minute. Stir in wine and simmer, stirring occasionally, until nearly evaporated, 8 to 10 minutes.

5. Stir in processed tomatoes, water, and prepared spaghetti squash. Remove from heat and season with sea salt and pepper to taste. Serve.

Pasta with Chicken and Broccoli

SERVES 6

Ingredients

Sea salt and pepper to taste

1 pound boneless, skinless chicken breasts, trimmed of all visible fat, halved lengthwise and sliced crosswise into ¼-inch-thick pieces

1 tablespoon coconut oil

1 onion, chopped fine

½ cup oil-packed, sun-dried tomatoes, rinsed, patted dry, and sliced ¼-inch thick

8 garlic cloves, minced

3 anchovy fillets, rinsed and minced

¼ teaspoon red pepper flakes

2 tablespoons tapioca or arrowroot flour

3 cups Chicken Broth or Stock (see page 236)

1 pound broccoli florets, cut into 1-inch pieces

1 pound Spaghetti Squash, prepared (see page 59)

1 ounce Coconut Milk Cheddar Cheese, grated (see page 239)

¼ cup chopped fresh basil

Preparation

1. Pat chicken dry with paper towels and season with sea salt and pepper. Heat two teaspoons oil in twelve-inch skillet over medium-high heat until just smoking. Add chicken and cook until browned and cooked through, about 5 minutes; transfer to bowl.

2. Add onion, sun-dried tomatoes, garlic, anchovies, pepper flakes, and remaining one teaspoon oil to fat left in skillet, cover, and cook over medium-low heat until onion begins to soften, about 5 minutes. Uncover, stir in flour, and cook for 1 minute. Slowly whisk in broth and simmer, covered, until tomatoes are softened, about 2 minutes. Remove lid and simmer until sauce has thickened, about 5 minutes. Remove from heat and stir in cooked chicken; cover until needed.

3. Meanwhile, bring four quarts of water to boil in large pot. Add broccoli and one tablespoon sea salt and cook until broccoli is bright green and tender, but still crisp in center, about 2 minutes; using a slotted spoon, transfer to large paper towel-lined plate.

4. Place spaghetti squash in bowl. Stir in chicken mixture, cooked broccoli, cheese, and basil. Cover and allow to sit for 1 minute. Season with sea salt and pepper to taste. Serve.

Shrimp Scampi with Pasta

SERVES 6

Ingredients

Sea salt and pepper to taste

1 onion, chopped fine

1 teaspoon olive oil

8 garlic cloves, minced

2 teaspoons minced fresh thyme

⅛ teaspoon red pepper flakes

2 cups Chicken Broth or Stock (see page 236)

2 (8-ounce) bottles clam juice

1 bay leaf

2 tablespoons tapioca or arrowroot flour

2 tablespoons water

½ cup fresh lemon juice (3 lemons)

1½ ounces Coconut Milk Cheddar Cheese, softened (see page 239)

1½ pounds extra-large shrimp, wild-caught, peeled, deveined, and tails removed

1 pound Spaghetti Squash, prepared (see page 59)

2 tablespoons minced fresh parsley

Preparation

1. Combine onion, oil, and sea salt in a twelve-inch nonstick skillet, cover, and cook over medium-low heat until softened, 8 to 10 minutes. Stir in garlic, thyme, and pepper flakes and cook until fragrant, about 30 seconds. Stir in broth, clam juice, and bay leaf and simmer until sauce has reduced to about two cups, 7 to 10 minutes.

2. Remove from heat and whisk in lemon juice and cheese until smooth. Stir in shrimp, cover, and let sit off heat until shrimp are cooked through, 7 to 10 minutes. Remove bay leaf. Whisk tapioca and water together in a bowl, then whisk into sauce. Return to heat and simmer, whisking constantly, until thickened.

3. Serve shrimp on top of spaghetti squash.

Chef's Note: Shrimp come in a variety of sizes and are typically identified by count per pound. Use this chart determine which shrimp to purchase for the recipe. Shrimp per pound:

- 10 shrimp or less = Colossal
- 11 to 15 = Jumbo
- 16 to 20 = Extra-large
- 21 to 30 = Large
- 31 to 35 = Medium
- 36 to 45 = Small
- about 100 = Miniature

American Chop Suey

SERVES 6

Ingredients

Sea salt and pepper to taste

8 ounces white mushrooms, trimmed and chopped coarse

1 tablespoon coconut oil

1 onion, chopped fine

1 red bell pepper, stemmed, seeded, and chopped

1 celery rib, chopped

2 garlic cloves, minced

2 tablespoons Soy Sauce (see page 233)

1 tablespoon tomato paste

1 pound 93% lean ground beef

1 (15-ounce) can tomato sauce

1 (14.5-ounce) can diced tomatoes

1½ cups Chicken Broth or Stock (see page 236)

8 ounces Spaghetti Squash, prepared (see page 59)

Preparation

1. Pulse mushrooms in a food processor until finely ground, about 10 pulses. Heat oil in a Dutch oven over medium heat until shimmering. Add processed mushrooms, onion, bell pepper, celery, and ¼ teaspoon sea salt and cook until vegetables begin to soften, about 5 minutes.

2. Stir in garlic, Soy Sauce, and tomato paste and cook until fragrant, about 1 minute. Stir in beef, breaking up meat with a wooden spoon, and cook until no longer pink, about 5 minutes. Stir in tomato sauce, diced tomatoes with their juices, and broth, scraping up any browned bits. Cover, reduce heat to low, and simmer until beef and vegetables are tender, about 20 minutes.

3. Plate beef and vegetable mixture atop spaghetti squash. Season with sea salt and pepper to taste and serve.

Pork Lo Mein

SERVES 6

Ingredients

½ tablespoon Soy Sauce (see page 233)

3 tablespoons Hoisin Sauce (see page 234)

2 tablespoons olive oil

¼ teaspoon five-spice powder

1 (1½-pound) pork tenderloin, trimmed of all visible fat, halved lengthwise, and sliced crosswise into ⅛-inch-thick pieces

¾ cup Chicken Broth or Stock (see page 236)

1½ teaspoons tapioca or arrowroot flour

12 ounces spaghetti squash

½ teaspoon coconut oil

6 tablespoons dry sherry

12 ounces shiitake mushrooms, stemmed and halved if small or quartered if large

½ head Napa cabbage, cored and sliced crosswise into ½-inch-thick pieces (6 cups)

8 scallions, white parts sliced thin, green parts cut into 1-inch pieces

1 tablespoon grated fresh ginger root

3 garlic cloves, minced

1 teaspoon Louisiana-Style Fermented Hot Sauce (see page 226)

Preparation

1. Combine Soy Sauce, Hoisin Sauce, olive oil, and five-spice powder together in a bowl. Measure ¼ cup sauce mixture into a separate bowl and stir in pork; cover and refrigerate for 30 to 60 minutes. Whisk broth and tapioca or arrowroot flour into remaining sauce mixture.

2. Heat 1½ teaspoons coconut oil in a Dutch oven over high heat until just shimmering. Add half of pork, breaking up any clumps, and cook until lightly browned but not fully cooked, about 3 minutes. Stir in three tablespoons sherry and cook until liquid is nearly evaporated, about 1 minute. Transfer to a clean bowl. Repeat with 1½ teaspoons coconut oil, remaining pork, and remaining three tablespoons sherry.

3. Wipe now-empty pot clean, add remaining 1½ teaspoons coconut oil, and place over high heat until shimmering. Add mushrooms and cook until lightly browned, 4 to 6 minutes. Stir in cabbage and cook until wilted, about 2 minutes. Stir in scallions, ginger, and garlic and cook until fragrant, about 30 seconds.

4. Whisk sauce to recombine and add to pot. Stir in cooked pork and any accumulated juices and simmer until sauce has thickened slightly and pork is heated through, about 1 minute. Stir in prepared spaghetti squash and hot sauce. Serve.

Pad Thai

Ingredients

Sea salt

Lime wedges

8 ounces cabbage sliced into ¼-inch-wide
strips

2 tablespoons tamarind paste

Enough boiling water to cover cabbage

3 tablespoons fish sauce

3 tablespoons palm sugar

2 tablespoons coconut oil

1 tablespoon white balsamic vinegar

¼ teaspoon cayenne pepper

12 ounces medium shrimp, wild-caught
peeled, deveined, and tails removed

1 shallot, minced

3 garlic cloves, minced

2 large eggs, lightly beaten

6 ounces asparagus, tough ends removed
and cut on the bias

4 scallions, sliced thin on bias

¼ cup minced fresh cilantro

2 tablespoons roasted, unsalted almonds,
chopped

Preparation

1. Cover cabbage with boiling water in a large pot and cover. Let cabbage soak until softened, pliable, and crisp-tender, about 1 minute; drain.

2. Meanwhile, soak tamarind paste in boiling water in a bowl until softened, about 10 minutes. Push mixture through a fine-mesh strainer into medium bowl, removing seeds and fibers and extracting as much pulp as possible. Whisk fish sauce, sugar, one tablespoon oil, vinegar, and cayenne into tamarind liquid.

3. Heat 1½ teaspoons oil in a twelve-inch nonstick skillet over high heat until shimmering. Add asparagus, shrimp, fish sauce mixture, and scallions. Cook for 2 to 3 minutes until shrimp are cooked through. Remove from skillet and set aside.

4. Add ½ tablespoon of oil to the now-empty twelve-inch nonstick skillet over medium-high heat. Add asparagus and stir-fry until crisp and tender. Remove from skillet and set aside.

5. Add remaining 1½ teaspoons oil to skillet and return to medium heat until shimmering. Add shallot and garlic and cook until lightly browned, about 1½

minutes. Stir in eggs and cook, stirring constantly, until scrambled but still moist, about 20 seconds. Stir in cabbage and sauce mixture; increase heat to high and cook, tossing gently, until cabbage is evenly coated, about 1 minute.

6. Stir in cooked shrimp, asparagus, and scallions and cook until shrimp are heated through and cabbage is tender, about 2 minutes. Season with sea salt to taste. Sprinkle with cilantro and almonds. Serve, passing lime wedges separately.

Chef's Note: Shrimp come in a variety of sizes and are typically identified by count per pound. Use this chart determine which shrimp to purchase for the recipe.

Shrimp per pound:
- 10 shrimp or less = Colossal
- 11 to 15 = Jumbo
- 16 to 20 = Extra-large
- 21 to 30 = Large
- 31 to 35 = Medium
- 36 to 45 = Small
- about 100 = Miniature

{ Casseroles and One-Dish Meals }

Chicken Divan

Ingredients

1 pound broccoli florets, frozen, cut into 1-inch pieces

1 tablespoon coconut oil

1 onion, chopped fine

2 garlic cloves, minced

1 teaspoon minced fresh thyme

Sea salt and pepper to taste

3 cups Chicken Broth or Stock (see page 236)

2 (12-ounce) cans coconut milk

½ cup water

1 tablespoon arrowroot or tapioca starch

1½ pounds boneless, skinless chicken breasts, trimmed of all visible fat, halved lengthwise, and cut into ½-inch-thick slices on bias

2 tablespoons Dijon Mustard (see page 225)

8 ounces Coconut Milk Cheddar Cheese, shredded (see page 239)

1 cup White Sandwich Breadcrumbs, toasted (see page 19)

Preparation

1. Adjust oven rack to middle position and preheat oven to 400° F. Grease a 13x9-inch baking dish.

2. Combine broccoli and ¼ cup water in a bowl, cover, and microwave until broccoli is tender, about 2 to 3 minutes. Drain broccoli and transfer to prepared baking dish.

3. Meanwhile, heat two teaspoons oil in a Dutch oven over medium heat until shimmering. Add onion, garlic, thyme, and one teaspoon sea salt and cook until onions are softened and lightly browned, 5 to 7 minutes. Whisk in broth and coconut milk and bring to a simmer. Stir in chicken and cook until no longer pink (chicken will not be fully cooked), about 4 minutes.

4. Remove from heat and stir in Dijon Mustard, ¼ teaspoon pepper, and cheddar, a handful at a time, until melted. Combine water and tapioca or arrowroot starch in a bowl and whisk to combine. Add tapioca mixture to chicken, place Dutch oven back on stove over medium-high heat, and stir until thickened.

5. Pour chicken mixture over broccoli in baking dish. Toss toasted breadcrumbs with remaining one teaspoon oil in bowl, season with sea salt and pepper to taste, and sprinkle over top. Bake until sauce is bubbling around edges, 15 to 20 minutes. Allow to cool slightly before serving.

Chicken Florentine

SERVES 4

Ingredients

4 teaspoons coconut oil

12 ounces baby spinach, fresh or frozen

1½ pounds boneless, skinless chicken breasts, trimmed of all visible fat

Sea salt and pepper to taste

1 shallot, minced

2 garlic cloves, minced

1 tablespoon tapioca or arrowroot starch

2 cups Chicken Broth or Stock (see page 236)

1¼ cups water

2 tablespoons coconut milk

1 teaspoon grated lemon zest

1 teaspoon lemon juice

2 tablespoons Coconut Milk Cheddar Cheese, grated (see page 239)

Preparation

1. Heat two teaspoons oil in a twelve-inch skillet over medium heat until shimmering. Add spinach, a handful at a time, and cook, stirring often, until wilted, about 5 minutes. Transfer spinach to a colander and press with a rubber spatula to remove excess liquid. Alternatively, use thawed frozen spinach, pressed dry through a colander.

2. Pat chicken dry with paper towels and season with sea salt and pepper. Wipe out now-empty skillet with paper towels, add remaining two teaspoons oil, and heat over medium-high heat until very hot. Brown lightly on both sides, 4 to 6 minutes total; transfer to a plate.

3. Add shallot and garlic to oil left in skillet and cook over medium heat until fragrant, about 30 seconds. Add broth and one cup of the water, scraping up any browned bits. Add browned chicken and any accumulated juices and bring to a simmer. Reduce heat to medium-low and cook until chicken registers 160° F, about 10 minutes. Transfer chicken to a carving board and tent loosely with aluminum foil.

4. Meanwhile, continue to simmer sauce until slightly thickened and reduced to ¾ cup, about 15 minutes. Whisk tapioca flour into remaining ¼ cup water in a small bowl and set aside. Remove from heat, whisk in coconut milk and

lemon zest and juice. Whisk in tapioca starch and water mixture and stir until thickened. Season with sea salt and pepper to taste.

5. Adjust oven rack to a position five inches from broiler element and heat broiler. Slice chicken crosswise into half-inch-thick slices and arrange slices in a two-quart, broiler-safe baking dish. Scatter spinach over top, then cover with sauce and sprinkle with cheese. Broil until cheese is spotty brown, about 30 seconds to 1½ minutes. Allow to cool slightly before serving.

Chicken Tetrazzini

SERVES 6

Ingredients

12 ounces boneless, skinless chicken breasts, trimmed of all visible fat and cut into ¾-inch pieces

1 teaspoon balsamic vinegar

5 ounces Spaghetti Squash, prepared (see page 59)

2 tablespoons coconut oil

1 tablespoon coconut milk

8 ounces white or cremini mushrooms, trimmed and sliced thin

1 onion, chopped fine

2 tablespoons coconut flour

2 cups Chicken Broth or Stock (see page 236)

2 tablespoons dry sherry

4 ounces Coconut Milk Cheddar Cheese, softened (see page 239)

1 ounce Coconut Milk Cheddar Cheese, grated (see page 239)

1 cup bell pepper, diced

½ cup White Sandwich Breadcrumbs, toasted (see page 19)

Preparation

1. Adjust oven rack to upper-middle position and preheat oven to 400° F. Combine chicken and vinegar in bowl, cover, and refrigerate for 30 minutes to one hour.
2. Meanwhile, melt oil in twelve-inch skillet over medium-high heat. Add mushrooms, onion, ½ teaspoon sea salt, and ½ teaspoon pepper and cook until browned.
3. Add flour, broth, and sherry to a medium-sized bowl and whisk to combine. Add mixture to skillet, scraping up any browned bits, and bring to a simmer. Whisk in coconut milk and four ounces cheese and simmer until slightly thickened, about 1 minute. Stir in marinated chicken and peppers and simmer gently for 1 minute (chicken will not be fully cooked). Add mixture to cooked spaghetti squash and toss to combine.
4. Transfer mixture to an eight-inch square baking dish. Toss toasted breadcrumbs with remaining cheese in a bowl, season with sea salt and pepper to taste, and sprinkle over top. Bake until hot throughout, 12 to 14 minutes. Allow to cool slightly before serving.

Chicken Pot Pie

SERVES 8

Ingredients

Coconut oil for greasing baking dish

1 Recipe Hearty Rustic Dough (See page 20)

½ cup arrowroot or tapioca flour

2 teaspoons coconut oil

1 onion, chopped fine

1 celery rib, minced

3½ cups Chicken Broth or Stock (see page 236)

1 teaspoon balsamic vinegar

2 pounds boneless, skinless chicken breasts, trimmed of all visible fat

3 carrots, peeled, halved lengthwise, and sliced ¼-inch thick

1 cup coconut milk

¾ cup frozen spinach, thawed and drained, or seasonally available greens

2 tablespoons minced fresh parsley

2 teaspoons fresh lemon juice

Sea salt and pepper to taste

2 egg whites, whisked until fluffy

Preparation

1. The evening before, prepare rustic dough starter in oven.
2. Prepare rustic dough and set aside. Adjust oven rack to middle position and preheat oven to 425° F. Grease a 13x9-inch rectangle dish with coconut oil.
3. Heat two teaspoons coconut oil in a Dutch oven over medium heat until shimmering. Add onion and celery and cook until softened and lightly browned, 8 to 10 minutes. Stir in broth and balsamic vinegar, scraping up any browned bits. Add chicken and carrots and bring to a simmer. Reduce heat to low, cover, and cook until chicken registers 160° F on meat thermometer. Transfer chicken to a carving board, cool slightly, and shred into bite-size pieces.
4. Whisk milk into tapioca flour until smooth, then whisk into pot. Bring to a simmer and cook, whisking constantly, until sauce thickens. Remove from heat and stir in shredded chicken, spinach, parsley, and lemon juice. Season with sea salt and pepper to taste.
5. Transfer mixture to prepared baking dish. Spoon rustic dough in dollops over top of chicken mixture and press into an even layer with greased hands. Brush top with reserved egg whites. Bake until dough is deep golden and sauce is bubbling around edges, about 15 minutes. Allow to cool slightly before serving.

Hearty Rustic Dough

MAKES 12 ROLLS

Ingredients

20 ounces unroasted/raw cashews, cashew pieces, or slivered almonds

½ cup plus 2 tablespoons filtered water

Enough probiotic capsules to equal about 30-40 billion strains

4 large eggs, separated

1 teaspoon baking soda

½ teaspoon sea salt

Coconut oil for greasing pan

Preparation

1. In a food processor, blend together the cashews or almonds and ½ cup filtered water until very smooth. Stop and stir as needed to keep the mixture moving, as it will be quite thick. Be patient; this could take up to 10 minutes depending on your processor. You don't want it to be grainy. Transfer to a non-reactive bowl (such as glass or ceramic); add the probiotic powder and stir until well combined. The mixture will be thick.

2. Cover the bowl with a plate. Place it in the middle of your oven with the oven light on. Do NOT turn the oven on. The light will create a slightly warm environment and allow the probiotics to become active. Leave in oven for twelve to twenty hours; the longer it sits, the more sour it will become. I make mine between 6:00 and 7:00 p.m. and bake the bread the next day between 11:00 a.m. and noon.

3. Transfer the cashew or almond mixture to a larger bowl. Take care to get as much of it transferred as possible. Using a rubber spatula works best for this.

4. Separate the egg yolks from the whites, putting the egg whites into a medium-sized bowl. Add the sea salt, yolks, and 2 tablespoons of water to the cashew mixture and beat until smooth and lump-free.

5. Rinse and dry the beaters so they're ready to beat the egg whites. Just before beating the egg whites, stir the sea salt and baking soda into the cashew mixture.

6. Using a hand mixer, beat the egg whites until soft peaks form. Gently fold them into the batter until the egg whites are no longer visible.

7. Grease a twelve-cup muffin tin with coconut oil. Pour equal quantities of batter into each of the tins, filling the cups two-thirds full. Brush with egg wash, place in oven, and bake for 15 to 17 minutes at 350° F. They are done when a toothpick inserted comes out clean.

Tuna Noodle Casserole

SERVES 8

Ingredients

Coconut oil for greasing baking sheet and baking dish

Sea salt and pepper to taste

12 ounces julienned zucchini or prepared spaghetti squash (see page 59)

3 (5-ounce) cans solid white tuna in water, drained thoroughly

2 teaspoons olive oil

2 teaspoons coconut oil, divided

2 teaspoons fresh-squeezed lemon juice

10 ounces white mushrooms, trimmed and sliced ¼-inch thick

1 onion, chopped fine

3 cups Chicken Broth or Stock (see page 236)

1½ cups coconut milk

½ cup water

2 tablespoons tapioca or arrowroot flour

7 ounces Coconut Milk Cheddar Cheese, shredded (see page 239)

1 cup frozen spinach, thawed and drained

1 cup White Sandwich Breadcrumbs, toasted (see page 19)

Preparation

1. Adjust oven rack to middle position and preheat oven to 425° F. Grease a 9x13-inch baking dish.

2. Combine tuna, two teaspoons olive oil, lemon juice, ¼ teaspoon sea salt, and ¼ teaspoon pepper in a bowl and flake tuna into coarse pieces with fork; let sit for 10 minutes. Julienne zucchini to create "noodles." Place "noodles" on lightly greased baking sheet. Sprinkle lightly with sea salt and pepper. Place in oven and bake for 5 to 10 minutes or until noodles release much of their moisture but aren't overcooked or burned. Remove and set aside. Or instead of zucchini, you can use prepared spaghetti squash and skip this oven step.

3. Over medium-high heat, heat one teaspoon coconut oil in a nonstick skillet until shimmering. Add mushrooms and onion and cook until liquid evaporates and mushrooms are browned, 5 to 7 minutes. Whisk in broth and coconut milk, scraping up any browned bits, and bring to a simmer. Combine water and arrowroot or tapioca in bowl, then whisk into pot. Continue to simmer, whisking

constantly, until sauce is slightly thickened, about 3 minutes. Remove from heat and whisk in cheese, a handful at a time, until melted. Stir in cooked zucchini noodles or prepared spaghetti squash, tuna mixture, spinach, ½ teaspoon sea salt, and ½ teaspoon pepper.

4.   Transfer mixture to prepared baking dish. Toss toasted breadcrumbs with remaining one teaspoon melted coconut oil in a bowl, season with sea salt and pepper to taste, and sprinkle over top of tuna mixture. Bake until sauce is bubbling around edges, 12 to 14 minutes. Allow to cool slightly before serving.

Mexican Lasagna

SERVES 8

Ingredients

Coconut oil for greasing baking dish and baking sheet

Sea salt and pepper to taste

2 teaspoons coconut oil

2 red bell peppers, stemmed, seeded, and cut into ½-inch pieces

1 onion, chopped fine

3 garlic cloves, minced

1 tablespoon minced canned chipotle chilies in adobo sauce (paleo-friendly)

2 teaspoons chili powder

1 pound ground turkey

2 cups Chicken Broth or Stock (see page 236)

1 (15-ounce) package frozen spinach, thawed and drained

2 cups poblano peppers (mild), chopped

1 (14.5-ounce) can diced tomatoes, drained

6 tablespoons minced fresh cilantro

2 tablespoons fresh lime juice

2 medium zucchinis, peeled

3 ounces Coconut Milk Cheddar Cheese, shredded (see page 239)

Preparation

1. Grease a 9x13-inch baking dish and baking sheet.

2. Using a mandolin, slice zucchini into ⅛-inch-thick slices. (Slice the zucchini lengthwise to make long "noodles"). Place on a greased baking sheet and bake in oven at 400° F until zucchini has released much of its moisture but isn't overcooked or burnt. Remove from oven and set aside.

3. Heat oil in a Dutch oven over medium heat until shimmering. Add bell peppers, onion, and ½ teaspoon sea salt, cover, and cook until softened, 5 to 7 minutes. Stir in garlic, chipotle, chili powder, and ¼ teaspoon pepper and cook until fragrant, about 30 seconds. Stir in turkey and cook, breaking up meat with a wooden spoon, until no longer pink, 5 to 8 minutes.

4. Gradually stir broth and bring to a simmer. Stir in spinach, poblanos, and tomatoes and simmer until mixture is slightly thickened and flavors have blended, about 10 minutes. Remove from heat, stir in ¼ cup cilantro and lime juice, and season with sea salt and pepper to taste.

5. Spread one-third of the turkey mixture into prepared baking dish. Cover with half of the baked zucchini, overlapping as needed, and sprinkle with one ounce of cheese. Repeat with half of remaining filling, remaining zucchini, and one ounce of cheese. Spread remaining filling over top and sprinkle with remaining ounce of cheese.

6. Bake until sauce is bubbling around edges, about 10 minutes. Allow to cool slightly and sprinkle with remaining two tablespoons cilantro. Serve.

Chicken Chilaquiles Casserole

Ingredients

2 poblano peppers, stemmed, seeded, and chopped coarse

2 onions, chopped fine

2 teaspoons coconut oil

Sea salt and pepper to taste

¼ cup minced fresh cilantro

6 garlic cloves, minced

2 teaspoons minced canned chipotle chilies in adobo sauce (paleo-friendly)

1 (14.5-ounce) can whole peeled tomatoes

¾ cup Chicken Broth or Stock (see page 236)

1½ pounds boneless, skinless chicken breasts, trimmed of all visible fat

3 ounces Coconut Milk Cheddar Cheese, crumbled (see page 239)

⅛ cup coconut milk

1 tablespoon lime juice

1 tomato, cored, seeded, and chopped

Preparation

1. Preheat oven to 350° F.
2. Combine poblanos, half of the onions, oil, and ¼ teaspoon sea salt in a twelve-inch skillet. Cover and cook over medium-low heat until vegetables are softened, 8 to 10 minutes. Uncover, increase heat to medium-high, and cook, stirring occasionally, until lightly browned, 4 to 6 minutes.
3. Stir in two tablespoons cilantro, garlic, and chipotle and cook until fragrant, about 30 seconds. Stir in canned tomatoes with their juices and the broth. Add chicken and bring to a simmer. Reduce heat to low, cover, and cook until chicken registers 160° F, 10 to 15 minutes.
4. Transfer chicken to a carving board, allow to cool slightly, then shred into bite-size pieces. Transfer sauce left in skillet to a blender and process until smooth, about 1 minute. Return sauce to skillet, season with sea salt and pepper to taste, and bring to a simmer over medium heat. Remove from heat and stir in shredded chicken. Transfer mixture to an eight-inch square baking dish and sprinkle with cheese. Bake on lower-middle rack until hot throughout, 5 to 10 minutes.
5. Allow casserole to cool slightly. Combine coconut milk and lime juice and drizzle over top, then sprinkle with tomato, remaining onions, and remaining two tablespoons cilantro. Serve.

King Ranch Casserole

SERVES 8

Ingredients

Coconut oil for greasing baking sheet

2-3 medium zucchinis

¼ cup almond flour

½ teaspoon granulated garlic

½ teaspoon chili powder

Sea salt and pepper

2 teaspoons coconut oil

2 onions, chopped fine

2 jalapeño chilies, stemmed, seeded, and minced

2 teaspoons ground cumin

2 (10-ounce) cans tomatoes with green chilies

3½ cups Chicken Broth or Stock (see page 236)

1½ pounds boneless, skinless chicken breasts, trimmed of all visible fat

⅛ cup coconut milk

6 tablespoons tapioca or arrowroot flour

6 ounces Coconut Milk Cheddar Cheese, shredded (see page 239)

2 tablespoons minced fresh cilantro

Preparation

1. Adjust oven racks to upper-middle and lower-middle positions and preheat oven to 450° F. Grease baking sheet.

2. Place almond flour, granulated garlic, chili powder, and ½ teaspoon sea salt in bowl and whisk to combine; set aside.

3. Using a mandolin, slice zucchini ⅛-inch thick. Place on greased baking sheet in a single layer and bake until zucchini releases most of its moisture but is not overcooked or burnt.

4. Heat oil in a Dutch oven over medium-high heat until shimmering. Add onions, jalapeños, and cumin and cook until lightly browned, about 6 minutes. Stir in tomatoes with their juices and cook until most of the liquid has evaporated, about 8 minutes. Stir in flour, ½ teaspoon sea salt, and ½ teaspoon pepper and cook for 1 minute. Slowly whisk in broth and bring to boil. Reduce heat to medium-low and simmer until thickened, about 3 minutes.

5. Add chicken and bring to a simmer. Reduce heat to low, cover, and cook until chicken registers 160° F, 10 to 15 minutes. Transfer chicken to a carving board, cool slightly, then shred into bite-size pieces.

6. Whisk tapioca flour into coconut milk until well combined. Off heat, but while mixture is still hot, stir in coconut milk and add cheese, a handful at a time, until melted and thickened. Stir in cilantro and shredded chicken.

7. Place half of the baked zucchini into a 13x9-inch baking dish, then top with half of chicken mixture; repeat with remaining zucchinis and remaining chicken mixture. Sprinkle almond flour mixture over top and spray lightly with oil spray. Bake on upper-middle rack until sauce is bubbling around edges, 15 to 20 minutes. Allow to cool slightly before serving.

Chicken Enchiladas

SERVES 4

Ingredients

Coconut oil for greasing baking dish

1 onion, chopped fine

1 teaspoon coconut oil

 Sea salt and pepper

3 garlic cloves, minced

3 tablespoons chili powder

2 teaspoons ground cumin

2 teaspoons palm sugar or honey
   (optional)

1 (15-ounce) can tomato sauce

1¼ cups water

1 pound boneless, skinless chicken breasts,
   trimmed of all visible fat

8 ounces Coconut Milk Cheddar Cheese,
   shredded (see page 239)

1 (4-ounce) can jalapeño chilies, drained
   and chopped

½ cup minced fresh cilantro

Preparation

1. Adjust oven rack to middle position and preheat oven to 350° F. Grease a 9x13-inch baking dish with coconut oil.

2. Combine onion, oil, and ½ teaspoon sea salt in a large saucepan, cover, and cook over medium-low heat until softened, 8 to 10 minutes. Stir in garlic, chili powder, cumin, and sugar and cook until fragrant, about 30 seconds. Stir in tomato sauce and water, bring to a simmer, and cook until slightly thickened, about 5 minutes. Add chicken and bring to a simmer. Reduce heat to low, cover, and cook until chicken registers 160° F, 10 to 15 minutes.

3. Transfer chicken to a carving board, cool slightly, then shred into small pieces. Strain sauce through a medium-mesh strainer into a bowl and press to extract as much liquid as possible. Transfer strained bits to a large bowl and stir in shredded chicken, ½ cup strained sauce, one cup cheese, jalapeños, and cilantro. Season chicken filling and sauce with sea salt and pepper to taste.

4. Place chicken in prepared baking dish, sprinkle with remaining cheese, and bake 10 to 15 minutes or until thick and bubbly. Allow to cool slightly before serving.

Shepherd's Pie

SERVES 6

Ingredients

1½ pounds lean ground beef

2 tablespoons plus 2 teaspoons water

½ teaspoon baking soda

 Sea salt and pepper to taste

2½ pounds turnips, peeled and cut into
    1-inch chunks

2 tablespoons olive oil

½ cup coconut milk

1 large egg yolk

8 scallions, green parts only, sliced thin

2 teaspoons coconut oil

1 onion, chopped

4 ounces white mushrooms, trimmed and
    chopped

1 tablespoon tomato paste

2 garlic cloves, minced

2 tablespoons Madeira or ruby port

2 tablespoons tapioca or arrowroot flour

1¼ cups Beef Broth or Stock (see page 236)

2 teaspoons Worcestershire Sauce
    (see page 230)

1 bay leaf

2 sprigs fresh thyme

2 carrots, peeled and chopped

2 teaspoons arrowroot or tapioca starch

Preparation

1. Grease a 9x13-inch baking dish with coconut oil. Toss ground beef with two tablespoons water, baking soda, one teaspoon sea salt, and ¼ teaspoon pepper in a bowl until well combined; set aside for 20 minutes.

2. Meanwhile, place turnips and one tablespoon sea salt in a large saucepan; add water to cover. Bring to a boil, then reduce to simmer and cook until turnips are tender, 8 to 10 minutes. Drain turnips and return to saucepan over low heat, stirring constantly, to evaporate any remaining moisture, about 1 minute. Remove from heat and mash turnips smooth with a potato masher. Stir in olive oil. Whisk milk and egg yolk together in a bowl, then stir into turnips. Stir in scallions; season with sea salt and pepper to taste. Cover; set aside.

3. Heat oil in a broiler-safe ten-inch skillet over medium heat until shimmering. Add onion and mushrooms and cook until vegetables begin to soften, 4 to 6 minutes. Stir in tomato paste and garlic and cook until bottom of skillet is dark brown, about 2 minutes. Stir in Madeira, scraping up any browned bits, and cook until evaporated, about 1 minute. Stir in flour and cook for 1 minute. Stir in broth, Worcestershire Sauce, bay leaf, thyme, and carrots; bring to a boil, scraping up any browned bits. Set aside once thickened.

4. Divide beef into two-inch pieces and place in a skillet over medium high heat. Cover and cook until beef is cooked through, 10 to 12 minutes, stirring and breaking up meat chunks with two forks halfway through cooking time. Combine arrowroot or tapioca and remaining two teaspoons water in a bowl, then stir into skillet. Continue to simmer; stirring constantly, until filling is slightly thickened, about 30 seconds. Remove thyme and bay leaf. Season with pepper to taste.

5. Place meat mixture in prepared baking dish. Spread turnip mash evenly over top of beef mixture. Adjust oven rack to a position six inches from broiler element and heat broiler. Broil until turnips are golden and sauce is bubbling, 10 to 15 minutes. Allow to cool slightly; serve.

Crustless Cheeseburger Pie

SERVES 6

Ingredients

Coconut oil for greasing pie pan

4 ounces Coconut Milk Cheddar Cheese, shredded (see page 239)

1 teaspoon coconut oil

1 onion, chopped fine

2 garlic cloves, minced

1 pound lean ground beef

3 tablespoons coconut flour

¾ cup Chicken Broth or Stock (see page 236)

2 tablespoons Ketchup (see page 221)

2 teaspoons Worcestershire Sauce (see page 230)

1 teaspoon Mustard (see page 222)

Sea salt and pepper

⅓ cup pickle slices

1 tomato, cored, seeded, and sliced thin

Preparation

1. Adjust oven rack to middle position and preheat oven to 400° F. Grease a nine-inch pie plate with coconut oil.

2. Heat oil in a twelve-inch nonstick skillet over medium heat until shimmering. Add onion, cover, and cook until softened and lightly browned, about 5 minutes. Uncover, stir in garlic, and cook until fragrant, about 1 minute. Stir in ground beef and cook, breaking up meat with a wooden spoon, until almost cooked through but still slightly pink, about 5 minutes. Stir in coconut flour and cook for 1 minute.

3. Gradually whisk in broth, Ketchup, Worcestershire Sauce, and Mustard. Bring to a simmer over medium-low heat and cook, stirring occasionally, until thickened, 3 to 5 minutes. Season with sea salt and pepper to taste.

4. Transfer mixture to prepared pie plate and top with pickles, tomato, and remaining cheese. Bake until cheese is melted and edges are browned, 10 to 12 minutes. Allow to cool slightly before serving.

Meat and Cheese Eggplant Lasagna

SERVES 10

Ingredients

Coconut oil for greasing baking sheet, baking dish, and foil

Sea salt and pepper to taste

1 onion, chopped fine

1 teaspoon olive oil

½ teaspoon ground rosemary

6 garlic cloves, minced

2 tablespoons tomato paste

¼ teaspoon dried oregano

¼ teaspoon red pepper flakes

1 pound ground chicken

1 (28-ounce) can crushed tomatoes

1 (28-ounce) can diced tomatoes, drained

1 cup chopped fresh basil

12 ounces Coconut Milk Cheddar Cheese, shredded (see page 239)

1 large egg, lightly beaten

2 medium or 4-6 small eggplants

Preparation

1. Preheat oven to 375° F. Grease a rimmed baking sheet with coconut oil. Peel eggplants and, using a mandolin, slice lengthwise into quarter-inch-thick slices. Place in a single layer, sprinkle with sea salt, pepper, and rosemary and bake for 8 to 10 minutes. Remove from oven and set aside. Grease a 9x13-inch baking dish.

2. Combine onion, oil, and ½ teaspoon sea salt in a Dutch oven, cover, and cook over medium-low heat until softened, 8 to 10 minutes. Stir in garlic, tomato paste, oregano, and pepper flakes and cook until fragrant, about 30 seconds. Stir in ground chicken and cook, breaking up meat with a wooden spoon, until no longer pink, about 4 minutes. Stir in crushed tomatoes and diced tomatoes and simmer until sauce has thickened slightly, about 15 minutes. Remove from heat, stir in ½ cup basil, and season with sea salt and pepper to taste; cover and set aside.

3. Place remaining ½ cup basil, cheese, egg, ½ teaspoon sea salt, and ½ teaspoon pepper in a bowl and mix until smooth and well combined.

4. Adjust oven rack to middle position and preheat oven to 375° F. Spread 1½ cups sauce into prepared baking dish. Place layer of eggplant in dish, top each noodle evenly with three ounces of cheese mixture, then spoon one cup sauce over top; repeat layering twice more.

5. Spread remaining 1½ cups sauce evenly over eggplant and sprinkle with remaining cheese. Grease sheet of aluminum foil with coconut oil, cover baking dish, and bake until sauce is bubbling around edges, about 35 minutes. Remove foil and continue to bake until cheese is lightly browned, 10 to 15 minutes. Allow to cool slightly before serving.

Spinach Lasagna

Ingredients

Coconut oil for greasing baking dish and baking sheet

1 onion, chopped fine

1 teaspoon coconut oil

Sea salt and pepper to taste

4 garlic cloves, minced

3 cups coconut milk

2 bay leaves

½ teaspoon ground nutmeg

2 tablespoons arrowroot or tapioca

20 ounces frozen spinach, thawed, squeezed dry, and chopped fine

2 medium or 4-6 small eggplants

9 ounces Coconut Milk Cheddar Cheese, shredded (see page 239)

Preparation

1. Preheat oven to 375° F. Grease a rimmed baking sheet with coconut oil. Peel eggplants and, using a mandolin, slice lengthwise into quarter-inch-thick slices. Place in a single layer, sprinkle with sea salt, pepper, and rosemary and bake for 10 to 12 minutes. Remove from oven and set aside. Grease a 9x13-inch baking dish.

2. Adjust oven rack to middle position and preheat oven to 425° F. Combine onion, oil, and sea salt in large saucepan, cover, and cook over medium-low heat until softened, 8 to 10 minutes. Stir in garlic and cook until fragrant, about 30 seconds. Stir in 2¾ cups coconut milk, bay leaves, and nutmeg; bring to a simmer. Combine tapioca flour and remaining ¼ cup milk in a bowl, then whisk into pot. Continue to simmer, whisking constantly, until sauce is slightly thickened. Remove from heat and discard bay leaves. Stir in spinach and ½ cup of cheese and season with sea salt and pepper to taste; cover and set aside.

3. Spread a small quantity of sauce in the bottom of prepared baking dish. Lay a single layer of eggplant on top of the sauce. Sprinkle eggplant with a portion of the cheese and cover with a small quantity of sauce. Repeat layers until all of the eggplant is used. Top with a layer of cheese.

4. Grease sheet of aluminum foil with coconut oil, cover baking dish, and bake until bubbling around edges, about 20 minutes. Remove from oven, adjust oven rack to a position six inches from broiler element, and heat broiler. Remove foil; broil until cheese is spotty brown, about 5 minutes. Allow to cool slightly before serving.

{ Condiments }

Fruit Jam

MAKES 8 OUNCES OF JAM

Ingredients

---

3 cups frozen berries or dried fruit (blueberries, strawberries, raspberries, dried
   apricots, blackberries, etc.)
⅔ cup honey
1 to 2 tablespoons of fresh lemon juice (juice of about 1 lemon)

Preparation

1. Place a small saucepan over medium heat. Add frozen berries or fruit and
   simmer until juices begin to release from the fruit. Add honey and lemon juice.
   Mix well and simmer for 5 to 7 minutes, then reduce heat to medium-low heat
   and simmer for another 5 to 7 minutes, stirring occasionally. Reduce heat to low
   and simmer until desired thickness is achieved. Thickness of the jam will vary
   with the amount of cooking time.

Chef's Note: Use one kind of berry or combine the types you like. Feel free to add spices
like ginger, ground cayenne, or black pepper, etc. to add a little kick or twist to
your jams.

Mayonnaise

MAKES ABOUT 1¼ CUPS

Ingredients

2 egg yolks
1 tsp Mustard (optional; see page 222)
3 tsp lemon juice
½ cup olive oil
½ cup coconut oil, melted

Preparation

1. Place the egg yolks in a bowl (or blender/food processor) with the Mustard (optional) and one teaspoon of lemon juice. Whisk, blend, or process, drizzling oil in very slowly, until a stable emulsion forms. If you add the oil too quickly, the emulsion will "break" and you will not be able to reverse. Discard and start over.
2. While whisking vigorously (blender or food processor on low) add the oil very slowly.
3. When all the oil is incorporated and the mayonnaise is thick, add the remaining lemon juice and season to taste with sea salt and pepper.
4. Refrigerate leftover mayonnaise and use within twenty-four hours.

Chef's Notes: Create flavored mayonnaise by adding herbs, spices and lacto-fermented cucumbers or other vegetables, finely minced (see Lacto-Fermented Vegetables on page 218) or Lacto-Fermented Horseradish (see page 229).

Do not substitute coconut oil for olive oil in this recipe, or it will become hard in the refrigerator. If you decide to use only olive oil in the recipe (no coconut oil), use light or mild-flavored olive oil to keep the mayonnaise flavor in a range palatable for most people.

Tartar Sauce

SERVES 6

Ingredients

1 cup Mayonnaise (see page 214)

½ tablespoon lemon juice or apple cider vinegar

1 tablespoon minced onion

¼ teaspoon sea salt

¼ teaspoon garlic powder

½ teaspoon dried dill

Pinch of fresh parsley (optional)

Preparation

1. In a medium bowl, add all of the ingredients and whisk to combine.
2. Refrigerate for at least 30 minutes before serving or using in your favorite recipe. May be stored in an airtight container in the refrigerator for up to three days.

Chef's Note: To make a more traditional tartar sauce, a little more time is required. Just remove the lemon juice or vinegar and add two tablespoons of lacto-fermented cucumbers (see Lacto-Fermented Vegetables recipe on page 218) and one teaspoon of raw honey.

Lacto-Fermented Vegetables

Makes 1 quart

Ingredients

Sea salt

Seasonal garden vegetables

Pickling spices

Leaves for crispness (grape, horseradish, oak, black tea—yes, the kind you drink—or Mesquite leaves.)

Preparation

1. Prepare a brine using a ratio of two tablespoons of sea salt to one quart of water. If it is over 85° F in your kitchen, use only one tablespoon of sea salt. Stir well and set aside.
2. Chop vegetables into sticks or bite-sized pieces.
3. Gather flavorings—garlic, onions, fresh herbs, or your favorite pickling spices.
4. Add garlic, herbs, and spices to the bottom of your clean quart, half-gallon, or gallon jar.
5. Add crisping leaves to the jar.
6. Place chopped vegetables on top of flavorings, leaving at least two inches of headspace from the rim of the jar. Pour the brine over the vegetables so they are covered by at least one inch of liquid. Two to four inches is even better, but hard to achieve with quart jars.
7. Weight down your vegetables so they stay below the brine while fermenting. I have used small plates that will fit into the jar opening, inverted plastic jar lids, large cabbage leaves, root vegetables slices, or glass weights made specifically for this purpose.
8. Seal the jar tightly and allow to sit at 65° F to 85° F for ten days or more, depending on your flavor preference. The longer they ferment, the more sour they become.
9. During the earliest stages of fermentation, carbon dioxide is released. Check your jars once or twice a day to see if the lids are building up pressure. If you cannot press down on the canning lid as you normally would, very quickly and carefully burp your jar by slightly unscrewing the lid, allowing a bit of gas to escape, and screwing it back on quickly.

10. Once fermentation is complete, move jar to cold storage—a root cellar, a basement, a cool garage, or anywhere below 65° F. Or yes—a refrigerator.

These are old-fashioned, brined, fermented pickles. They keep for months, if prepared properly. And they're easy to prepare.

The process of lactic acid fermentation is part art and part science. You're probably familiar with the fermentation of cabbage to sauerkraut and kimchi. By the same biological process, we can make brine-pickled vegetables from whatever is in our seasonal garden.

The same beneficial organisms we find in healthy soil are on the surface of the vegetables we grow in that soil. Those beneficial organisms digest the carbohydrates in the vegetables and produce organic acids, as well as enzymes and beneficial bacteria that preserve the vegetables through a process we call fermentation. Fermentation produces a brine that is part lactic and part acetic, and naturally prevents the vegetables from spoiling. The reaction happens anaerobically, outside the presence of oxygen, which is why it's important to cover the vegetables in a sea salt brine. This is the most critical aspect of fermentation: You must keep your vegetables covered in brine.

The resulting flavor is mildly sour, tangy, and sometimes a little sweet, but rarely harsh. The differences you will note in store-bought pickles vs. lacto-fermented pickles is that store-bought are more sour. This is because of the vinegar brine used in the canning process. Lacto-fermented pickles are less sour, but oh-so-flavorful.

The recipe can be used for cucumbers, garlic, carrots, squash, radishes, asparagus, green tomatoes, and most other vegetables. The recipe is for a quart jar, but it can be easily scaled up or down to fit a pint, half-gallon or one-gallon vessel.

Ketchup

Ingredients

1 can (6 ounces) tomato paste

2 tablespoons apple cider vinegar, lemon juice, or lime juice

¼ teaspoon dry mustard powder

⅓ cup water

¼ teaspoon cinnamon

¼ teaspoon sea salt

1 pinch ground cloves

1 pinch ground allspice

⅛ teaspoon ground red pepper (optional)

Preparation

Combine all the ingredients in a bowl and whisk to combine. Place in refrigerator overnight to allow flavors to bloom. Serve cold or allow required quantity to come to room temperature before serving.

Mustard

Ingredients

½ cup dry mustard powder
¼ cup water
¼ cup white wine vinegar
Sea salt to taste

Preparation

1. Combine the mustard powder, water and vinegar in a bowl and whisk. Let stand for 30 minutes before using.

2. Use small quantities brushed on bread for sandwiches and as an ingredient in other recipes in this book.

3. This is a basic recipe that will not have the typical consistency of mustard. It's thinner than you would expect, but packed with flavor. So use judiciously! Add herbs and spices or Lacto-Fermented Horseradish to vary the flavor. Store in a glass jar with tight-fitting lid for up to one year in the refrigerator.

Dijon Mustard

Ingredients

¼ cup yellow mustard seeds

¼ cup brown mustard seeds

1 cup white balsamic vinegar

4 tsp dry mustard powder

¼ cup white wine vinegar

½ teaspoon sea salt

Preparation

1. Soak the mustard seeds in the white balsamic vinegar overnight.
2. Place the seeds and soaking liquid in a blender or food processor with the mustard powder, vinegar, and sea salt and process to a paste-like consistency.
3. Place in a glass jar, cover tightly, and refrigerate for four days before serving.

Chef's Notes: Adding your favorite fresh herbs, oven-roasted or sundried tomatoes, oven roasted peppers, fresh basil, or fresh oregano makes for exciting variations on this classic recipe.

Louisiana-Style Fermented Hot Pepper Sauce

MAKES ABOUT 1 PINT

Ingredients

---

1 pint loosely packed fresh red chili peppers, tops snipped and chilies sliced (use gloves; any red pepper will work, but cayenne are often used)

Enough sweet white wine (Riesling or similar) to completely cover the chili peppers with ½ inch of wine above the top surface of the peppers

Sea salt, 2% of the weight of your chili peppers (for example: 12 ounces of peppers would require 0.24 ounces of sea salt—use a digital kitchen scale to weigh sliced peppers and sea salt)

Sea salt to taste, for adding to the mash after fermentation (optional)

Preparation

1. Using gloves, pack chilies and sea salt in a glass canning jar, leaving 1½ inches of empty space between the top of the jar and the surface of the peppers.

2. Pour white wine over the chilies, completely covering the peppers, leaving about one inch of head space between the top of the liquid and the top of the jar. Using a small spoon, mash the peppers thoroughly in the jar. If it's too difficult to mash in the jar, perform this step in a large bowl and then transfer to the jar.

3. Cover the jar tightly with cheesecloth and wrap a rubber band around the cloth and neck of jar to hold the cloth in place. Or just use a canning jar ring and screw it on the jar over the cloth to hold it in place and protect the fermentation from dust and insects. Leave the jar in a cool place; 65 to 85° F. I leave mine on my kitchen counter.

4. Check the fermentation every morning for white mold. Remove the mold with a spoon. Using a clean spoon, stir the peppers and secure cloth cover. Repeat this exercise each day until the desired level of fermentation (taste) is reached, two to six weeks. Sauce will bubble as it ferments. When bubbling stops, sauce is fully fermented. You may stop it at any time after the two-week mark.

5. Once the Louisiana-Style Fermented Hot Pepper Sauce is fermented to your taste preferences, place a food mill over a bowl and pour the pepper mash and brine into the mill. Mill the flesh and seeds, rotating the handle of the mill in both directions to extract as much juice from the pepper mash as possible. Once as much of the mash has passed through the food mill as possible, discard the remains in the mill.

6. Measure the volume of the brine liquid and add half that amount of your favorite naturally fermented vinegar. Apple cider is an easily obtainable option and a good place to start. You may also add a little sea salt to the mash if you think the flavor is too simple and a little complexity is desired. Stir well, seal the jar, and store in the refrigerator for up to one year.

Lacto-Fermented Horseradish

MAKES ABOUT 1 CUP

Ingredients

1 cup horseradish root, peeled and grated
1 packet vegetable culture starter
Filtered and sterile water
1½ tsp sea salt

Preparation

1. Combine horseradish root, vegetable culture starter, and sea salt to a blender or food processor and pulse to combine ingredients.
2. Add water, one tablespoon at a time, pulsing the food processor or blender to incorporate. Add only enough water to create a paste.
3. Place the horseradish paste in a sterilized glass jar and add water to completely fill the jar. Place a loose-fitting lid over the top of the jar. Set the jar in a saucer and store in a warm place for three to seven days, or until horseradish is completely fermented. Seal lid tightly and store in the refrigerator for up to six months.

Chef's Notes: If you have children in your life, this is a great project to conduct with them. Use it as a way to teach them about healthy bacteria and how probiotics are an important part of a healthy digestive system.

The vegetable starter used in this recipe was acquired from a local health food store. You can also order a starter online. Just use the one that is easiest for you to acquire, fits your budget, and is suitable for fermentation of horseradish. I like to use a broad-range vegetable culture for multiple lacto-fermentation recipes.

Worcestershire Sauce

MAKES ABOUT 1¼ CUPS

Ingredients

½ cup apple cider or balsamic vinegar

2 tablespoons water

2 tablespoons Soy Sauce (see page 233)

¼ teaspoon ground ginger

¼ teaspoon dry mustard powder

¼ teaspoon onion powder

¼ teaspoon garlic powder

⅛ teaspoon ground cinnamon

⅛ teaspoon freshly ground black pepper

Preparation

Add all ingredients to a saucepan over medium heat and whisk to combine. Gently bring to a boil and reduce heat to low. Simmer for 15 minutes. Cool to room temperature. Transfer to a container with a tight-fitting lid and store in the refrigerator for up to six months.

Worcestershire Sauce is traditionally fermented, and a fermented version is healthier for you. However, this simple recipe tastes just as good and can be made with easy-to-find ingredients.

Soy Sauce

MAKES ABOUT ⅓ CUP OF SAUCE

Ingredients

12 tablespoons Beef Broth or Stock (see page 236)

4 teaspoons balsamic vinegar

2 teaspoons blackstrap molasses

¾ teaspoon grated ginger root

1 pinch white pepper

1 pinch garlic powder

1½ cups water

Preparation

1. In a saucepan over medium-high heat, add beef stock and bring to a boil. Continue to boil until the broth is reduced to a third of its original volume.

2. Add remaining ingredients to the saucepan and bring to a boil. Continue to gently boil until reduced to a quarter of its volume, about 15 minutes.

3. Remove from heat and cool the sauce to room temperature. Place in an airtight container and store in the refrigerator for up to thirty days.

Hoisin Sauce

MAKES ABOUT ¾ CUP OF SAUCE

Ingredients

4 tablespoons Soy Sauce (see page 233)

2 tablespoons almond butter

1 tablespoon blackstrap molasses or 1 tablespoon raw honey

2 teaspoons balsamic vinegar

1 garlic clove, finely minced

2 teaspoons olive oil

1 teaspoon Louisiana-Style Fermented Hot Pepper Sauce (see page 226)

⅛ teaspoon black pepper

Preparation

Combine all ingredients in a small mixing bowl and whisk to combine. Store in an air-tight container in the refrigerator for up to thirty days.

{ Meat & Poultry Stock }

Stock can be made from any animal bone, period. If you can eat it, cook it, and it has bones, save the bones, ask your butcher for bones, and get bones from your neighbors, coworkers, friends, and family members! Some people save bones for their animals; I save bones for my stock! Bones are very valuable when it comes to the liquid portion of most main course recipes.

There isn't a real need for precision when it comes to making stock. The most basic stock involves placing bones in cold water with a couple of tablespoons of vinegar and simmering low and slow until a rich bouquet of flavor develops. For richer stocks, roast bones first for 25 to 35 minutes in a 350 to375° F oven. Then place them in water with vinegar and simmer.

Never add sea salt to your stock. If you add sea salt now, you'll have less flexibility later when you are incorporating the stock into a sauce or soup that contains other savory ingredients. You can always add sea salt to the finished recipe, if desired.

No need to remove fat from stock, unless you're making chicken stock. Chicken fat contains polyunsaturated fats that will oxidize over time and ruin the stock.

Feel free to get creative and try different ingredients in your stock. Consider using herbs and spices and combining different types of animal bones in your stock.

How long does it take?
Allow around two hours for fish bones, four hours for chicken stock, and a minimum of six hours for tougher bones that come from pigs, cows, deer, bison, and elk. It's virtually impossible to overcook tougher bones. The longer they simmer, the more nutrients are extracted. I've cooked stocks for as long as two days. I don't usually let chicken or fish

bones go for more than one day because they tend to disintegrate. Remember to add water periodically to your stock to make sure it doesn't boil dry.

If you own a pressure cooker, you can make stock in under an hour! Just follow the instructions in your pressure cooker manual.

Store stock in freezer-safe containers and freeze for up to one year. Thaw before using in prepared recipes.

Mirepoix (vegetable stock)
A mirepoix is usually a mixture of aromatic vegetables or the "holy trinity" of French cooking: diced carrots, celery, and onions. The French use it in most flavoring liquids because they impart great taste and aroma (and we all know aroma is key to taste). If adding them to meat stocks, add them in last part of the cooking time to avoid disintegration. Filter out with the bones and discard when stock is finished cooking.

Bouquet Garni
A bouquet garni is a mixture of sturdy herbs like thyme, rosemary, and bay leaves. They are tied together or placed in a porous cloth pouch (often made of cheesecloth) and added to stocks. Consider adding fresh peppercorns, cinnamon, or other sturdy spices and herbs to your Bouquet Garni when making stocks.

Final Steps
Cool stock in the refrigerator (not at room temperature) before final storage. Allowing stock to cool at room temperature jump-starts bacterial growth and rapid reproduction. After cooling completely, package and freeze. Store stock you will use within five days in the refrigerator. If not used in that time frame, discard.
Before using stock in soups, sauces, and other applications, thaw the stock and boil for 10 minutes to sterilize and kill any bacteria living in the stock.

Coconut Milk Cheddar Cheese

MAKES ONE 8X4 LOAF PAN

Ingredients

2 cans coconut milk (full fat, Thai Kitchen brand preferred)

3 tablespoons agar flakes

1 teaspoon white balsamic vinegar

4 tablespoons tapioca starch

1 teaspoon smoked paprika

¼ teaspoon liquid smoke

2 teaspoons sea salt

¼ cup nutritional yeast flakes (gives more cheese flavor)

Pinch of turmeric (optional; provides cheese color)

Preparation

1. Grease a flat-bottomed dish or line a loaf pan with parchment paper.
2. Boil coconut milk, while whisking, until no longer separated. Add white balsamic vinegar, agar flakes, and sea salt. Whisking continuously, gently boil for 15 minutes.
3. Add remaining ingredients one at a time, whisking all the while. Cook for another 5 to 10 minutes.
4. Pour cheese into prepared pan.
5. Allow to cool for two hours. Place cooled cheese in refrigerator with plastic wrap pressed against the surface or with a lid on container. Use after eight to twelve hours of refrigeration. Refrigerated cheese can be grated, but it will be a little slippery.

Boursin Cheese

Ingredients

4 ounces Coconut Milk Cheddar Cheese (see page 239)

1 pinch garlic powder

1 pinch dried dill weed

1 pinch dried marjoram

1 pinch dried basil

1 pinch black pepper

1 pinch ground thyme

1 pinch dried parsley

Preparation

Add all ingredients to a bowl and mash together with a fork until thoroughly combined. Refrigerate in an airtight container for up to two weeks or until ready to use.

Marshmallows

MAKES ONE 8X8 PAN OF MARSHMALLOWS

Ingredients

1 cup water (divided equally)

3 tablespoons grass-fed beef gelatin

1 cup honey

1 teaspoon vanilla extract

¼ teaspoon salt

Coconut oil

Tapioca flour to coat the outside of the
marshmallows

Coconut oil for greasing foil

Preparation

1. Make a foil sling for an eight-inch square baking pan by folding two long sheets of aluminum foil so each is eight inches wide. Lay sheets of foil in pan perpendicular to each other, with extra foil hanging over edges of pan. Push foil into corners and up sides of pan, smoothing foil flush to pan. Grease foil with coconut oil and sprinkle with a thin layer of tapioca flour.

2. Add gelatin and ½ cup of the water to the bowl of a stand mixer.

3. While the gelatin is softening, combine remaining ½ cup of water, honey, and salt in a saucepan over medium heat. Bring the mixture to a boil. Place a candy thermometer in the saucepan and continue to boil the mixture until it reaches 242° F, the soft ball stage. Don't exceed 245° F.

4. When honey mixture reaches 240 to 242° F, immediately remove the saucepan from the heat.

5. Turn the stand mixer on low-medium speed and begin mixing the gelatin and water. Pour the honey mixture in a slow, steady stream down the side of the bowl, not pouring directly on the gelatin. It's critical to pour in this manner to prevent the hot honey mixture from "breaking" the gelatin, which will cause the marshmallow mixture to break up later when it's time to spread and form.

6. When the syrup and the gelatin are well combined, turn off the mixer and, using a spoon, give it a final stir.

Continued on following pages . . .

7. Turn the mixer speed to high and continue beating until mixture cools and becomes very thick, like marshmallow crème (7 to 10 minutes). Add vanilla during the last minute of mixing.
8. Transfer the marshmallow crème to the prepared pan with foil sling. Smooth the top.
9. Allow the marshmallows to stand at room temperature for one to six hours until they reach the desired firmness. If you want a clean look after cutting, wait at least four hours before cutting. Even if you think they are firm enough, wait!
10. Remove from pan using foil sling and fold down sides of foil. Cut marshmallows to the desired size, adding more tapioca flour while cutting to keep knife from sticking. Toss again in tapioca flour to give them a nice finish.
11. Using tapioca flour works well for coating marshmallows that will be used for roasting or topping dishes. It enables quicker drying times and aids in the browning process. Marshmallows intended for roasting should be cut and left at room temperature overnight, covered with cheesecloth. Then store the marshmallows in a sealed container in the refrigerator for five to seven days, or until needed.

Note: If you're making these at higher elevation, decrease the cooking temperature by 2° F per 1,000 feet. If your pot is too big, the honey syrup will be more likely to burn, as the temperature will rise too quickly and the thermometer may not read accurately. If the honey mixture foams, use a spoon to break up the foam so that it doesn't overflow, but do not stir the syrup.

{ Conversions and Equivalencies }

Ibelieve cooking is equal parts science and art, and your physical location has a lot to do with how to prepare a recipe. That is to say, the locations from which your ingredients originate have an impact on the overall recipe formulation. Ingredients from different parts of the world may vary slightly, and I cannot promise that almond flour from one supplier will yield exactly the same result as another. I can, however, offer guidelines for converting weights and measurements. I also recommend that you rely on your individual judgment (here's the art part) when preparing the recipes. If a recipe isn't behaving exactly as I describe it should, adjust the moisture, flours, or palm sugar levels until you get it right. The recipes in this book were developed using standard U.S. measures. The following charts offer equivalents for U.S., metric, and imperial (U.K.) measures. All conversions are approximate and have been rounded up or down to the nearest whole number.

EXAMPLE: 1 teaspoon = 4.9292 milliliters (rounded up to 5 milliliters) 1 ounce = 28.3495 grams (rounded down to 28 grams)

VOLUME CONVERSIONS U.S. TO METRIC
1 teaspoon = 5 milliliters
2 teaspoons = 10 milliliters
1 tablespoon = 15 milliliters
2 tablespoons = 30 milliliters
¼ cup = 59 milliliters
⅓ cup = 79 milliliters
½ cup = 118 milliliters
¾ cup = 177 milliliters
1 cup = 237 milliliters
1¼ cups = 296 milliliters

1½ cups = 355 milliliters
2 cups (1 pint) = 473 milliliters
2½ cups = 591 milliliters
3 cups = 710 milliliters
4 cups (1 quart) = 0.946 liter
1.06 quarts = 1 liter
4 quarts (1 gallon) = 3.8 liters

WEIGHT CONVERSIONS U.S. TO METRIC
Ounces To Grams
½ = 14
¾ = 21
1 = 28
1½ = 43
2 = 57
2½ = 71
3 = 85
3½ = 99
4 = 113
4½ = 128
5 = 142
6 = 170
7 = 198
8 = 227
9 = 255
10 = 283
12 = 340
16 (1 pound) = 454

OVEN TEMPERATURES: FAHRENHEIT TO CELSIUS AND TO GAS MARK (IMPERIAL)

225 = 105 = ¼
250 = 120 = ½
275 = 135 = 1
300 = 150 = 2
325 = 165 = 3
350 = 180 = 4
375 = 190 = 5
400 = 200 = 6
425 = 220 = 7
450 = 230 = 8
475 = 245 = 9

Subtract 32° F from the Fahrenheit reading, and then divide the result by 1.8 to find the Celsius reading.

Temperature conversion example:
175° F − 32 = 143°
143° ÷ 1.8 = 79.44° C, rounded down to 79° C

{ Index }